Roadside Bicycle Repairs

The simple guide to fixing your bike

Rob Van der Plas

Illustrated by the author

Second, expanded and updated edition
Bicycle Books — San Francisco

Copyright	© Rob Van der Plas, 1987, 1990
	Second, expanded and updated edition, 1990
	Printed in the United States of America
Cover photograph	Neil van der Plas
Published by	Bicycle Books, Inc.
	P.O. Box 2038
	Mill Valley, CA 94941
Distributed to the book trade by	(USA) The Talman Co., New York, NY
	(Canada) Raincoast Book Distributing, Vancouver, BC
	(UK) Chris Lloyd Sales &Marketing Services, Poole, Dorset
Library of Congress Cataloging in Publication Data	Van der Plas, Robert, 1938 —
	Roadside Bicycle Repairs, The simple guide to fixing your bike (second edition)
	Bibliography: p. Includes Index. 1. Bicycles and bicycling, Handbooks, Manuals, etc. 2. Authorship I. Title.
	Library of Congress Catalog Card Number 89-81203
ISBN	0-933201-27-3
Note	The first edition appeared under ISBN 0-933201-16-8

Acknowledgements

Since the first edition of this book appeared in 1987, I have learned a lot — particularly about what to include and what to leave out, how to do certain jobs more easily, when to get professional help and how to explain certain operations. I would like to thank the many people who have helped me in this respect: It is only through their constructive criticism that this new edition forms a major improvement over the first.

In particular, I wish to thank Portia Masterson of Self Propulsion, Inc. for her very thorough review and exacting comments. If any errors still remain, it is certainly not due to my critics' oversights, but merely to my own stubbornness in sometimes adhering to my own way of saying things.

About the Author

Rob Van der Plas is a professional engineer and a lifelong cyclist. He commutes to work regularly and has both raced and toured by bicycle extensively in Europe and America. For many years now he has occupied himself primarily with the technical aspects of the bicycle. In this capacity he has taught bicycle repair and maintenance courses and made numerous contributions on the subject to specialized periodicals on both sides of the Atlantic.

In addition to the present book, Bicycle Books has published several of his other works, including *The Bicycle Touring Manual, The Bicycle Racing Guide, The Mountain Bike Book*, and *The Bicycle Repair Book*. And, yes, between writing books and articles on the subject, he still finds time to ride and maintain his bike.

Table of Contents

Chapter 8
Gearing
Problems 72

Chapter 9
Wheel
Problems 82

Chapter 1
Introduction

The present book is intended as a simple repair guide for those who are only marginally interested in the bicycle's technical details. It will keep you out of trouble by showing you how to handle the most frequently occurring problems that can happen while riding the bike. It is not a complete guide to the bicycle and its maintenance, but with the help of these instructions you will usually be able to get back on the bike quickly if anything does go wrong *en route*. Nothing more, nothing less. That, however, is what most novice cyclists — and quite a number of more experienced riders — need most of all.

Understanding the Bike

Of course, there is more to know about the bicycle, and specifically there is more to bicycle maintenance than can be covered in this slender volume. Preventive maintenance is the key to enjoyable cycling with a minimum number of mishap: the more preventive maintenance is carried out on the bike, the less likely you are to have to resort to this book when riding. For those who don't want to be bothered, the bike shop is the place to get the bike serviced regularly, particularly before any longer trip in difficult or remote terrain. For those who are interested in doing much of this work themselves, there are some excellent general bicycle books on the market, the most practical of which are referenced in the Bibliography in the back of the book.

A Simple Machine

The bicycle is a simple machine. Everything on it is light and relatively straightforward enough to be understood and overhauled by even the relatively non-technical person. So it is curious to observe that some technically skilled people panic when their bikes develop a problem. People who think nothing of taking their computer to pieces have been encountered helpless when faced with a flat tire or a skipping bike chain. Instead of repairing the bike, they try to hitch a ride home, essentially ruining a whole day for what is really only a minor operation that can be handled with simple tools in a matter of minutes.

All you need is a basic understanding of the bicycle's

components, a few simple tools and either an inquisitive mind or the advice contained in this book. Make sure you carry the tools and spares listed in Chapter 3, and find a place for this book in your bike bag or shirt pocket. It will be fun to know you can help yourself if anything should go wrong.

Choice of Words

This book is sold both in the US and in Britain, and this brings up the problem of what kind of English to use. I shall generally adhere to American English. However, I will provide the British term the first time it is used, wherever the two differ by more than the spelling alone. Thus, my British readers will have to get used to seeing *aluminum* right from the start, but they may find it useful to be told that a crankset is what they are used to calling a chain set and that a wrench is a spanner. Conversely, I must ask my American readers to put up with some of these explanations: they are not intended to teach them British English, but merely to help the British readers understand the American text.

At this point I should also say a few words about the use of the masculin and the feminin forms. Though I am as open to sexual equality as any male can possibly be expected to be, I use the masculin form where the words are used in their general sense. Thus, you will find terms like he and his, as opposed to clumsy constructions like *he/she* and *him/her,* not to mention the to my linguistic sensitivity monstrous compounds ending in *-person*. You are welcome to object to this kind of usage, but I have found it to be clearer and less confusing — even to most women.

About this Book

In the first four chapters, I shall address the general topics of bicycle care — those things that every cyclist should know about the bike, the way it works and the way it is maintained, before we will get down to the step-by-step instructions for solving individual mechanical problems starting in Chapter 5. In Chapter 2, I shall introduce the various kinds of bicycles and the parts that make them up. In Chapter 3, you will be shown the basic tools and other equipment to use for roadside repairs and preventive maintenance. Chapter 4 will show you how to treat your bike to prevent serious problems as much as possible.

In the remaining chapters of the book (chapters 5 through 11), you will find detailed instructions for handling specific repairs with which you may be confronted *en route*. Each of these instructions will be preceded by a brief text that helps you establish what is wrong and what must be done to solve the problem.

Be Prepared

Though you may be tempted to tuck the book in your bike bag and forget about it until you run into trouble, it will be smarter to take the trouble to do your homework first. In order to work competently on the bike, you should read and understand the first four chapters, and make yourself familiar with your bike's operation as well as the use of the various tools listed. Armed with that, you are well prepared to tackle anything — and if you follow the advice in Chapter 4 about preventive maintenance, very little will actually go wrong while you are out riding the bike.

Finally, I suggest you consciously evaluate the risks involved in certain of the makeshift repairs suggested in various places: if the risk of an accident is too great, walk the bike or hitch a ride home rather than risking a fast and dangerous descent on a patched-up machine.

Chapter 2
Know Your Bike

Fig. 2.1 Mountiain bike

Bicycle Types

Although in recent years only two basic models have constituted the majority of all bicycle sales — the ten-speed and the mountain bike — there are quite a number of different models on the market. They range from the real racing machine to the BMX-bike, from the old English three-speed to folders, and from cruisers to tandems. Though this book will emphasize the problems that are likely to occur with ten-speeds and mountain bikes, the instructions will apply equally to all other models.

In the following paragraphs, I shall briefly describe the various bikes available. That will be done in the form of an illustration and a brief text describing the most characteristic features of each model.

Mountain Bike and Hybrid

The mountain bike, illustrated in Fig. 2.1, is also known as ATB (all terrain bike). It has fat knobby tires, wide-range derailleur gearing with 18 or 21 speeds, an easily adjusted seat, and flat handlebars. The hybrid is similar, but has narrower wheels and usually slightly different handlebars.

Ten-Speed and Racing Bike

Fig. 2.2 Ten-speed bike

Ten-speed is the common name for all bikes with drop handlebars and derailleur gearing. In fact, most have 12 or more speeds these days. The ten-speed has a relatively narrow saddle and less wide-range gearing than the mountain bike. It is shown in Fig. 2.2.

The real racing bike is the most sophisticated version of the ten-speed. It looks similar but is made with the lightest materials and equipped with the most sophisticated components, including special wired-on tires, called sew-ups in the US, tubs in Britain.

Utility Bike, Cruiser and Three-Speed

This is the conventional American paperboy bike, shown in Fig. 2.3. It has a heavy welded frame and comes equipped with a coaster brake, fat tires and upright handlebars.

The cruiser is nothing more than a simple rugged bike that at first looks similar to either the old American utility bike or the mountain bike. It is distinguished from

Fig. 2.3 Utility bike

the former by having derailleur gearing and hand brakes, from the latter by being much heavier and offering less gearing choice and poorer brakes.

The three-speed is the British equivalent of the utility bike, equipped with three-speed hub gearing, flat or upright handlebars and fenders. Though they are getting rarer due to the advent of the mountain bike, they are still around.

Tandem

Fig. 2.4 Tandem

The tandem is the bicycle built for two, shown in Fig. 2.4. It has made a remarkable resurgence in recent years, though it will of course never be anything like as prominent as any single bike. It comes in versions akin to the ten-speed and in those that look more like the mountain bike.

Folding Bike

Though rare indeed in the US, the folding bicycle can be quite handy for the bicycle commuter who has to combine cycling with public transportation or car-pooling. It comes in a variety of different designs, only one of which is depicted in Fig. 2.5. Different models run the gamut from very simple to highly sophisticated.

BMX-Bike

The BMX-bike is more a toy, and often thought of as the kid's mountain bike. Actually, there are now also real mountain bikes available in children's sizes, and for getting around the latter are far more suitable, due to their better gearing and their more comfortable riding position.

Parts of the Bike

Whatever kind of bicycle you ride, it is built up similarly, though the various parts may look a little different on the one bike than on the other. Fig. 2.6 shows all the components of a typical ten-speed. It will be helpful for your handling of the bike and your understanding of the instructions that follow if you learn the names of the various components by heart and are able to identify them on your bike.

In addition to the fact that various parts may look different on different models, some bikes have hub gearing instead of the derailleur system depicted, or they may have a coaster brake instead of the rim brakes shown. Finally, some bikes come equipped with a num-

Fig. 2.5 Folding bike

Fig. 2.6 Parts of the bicycle

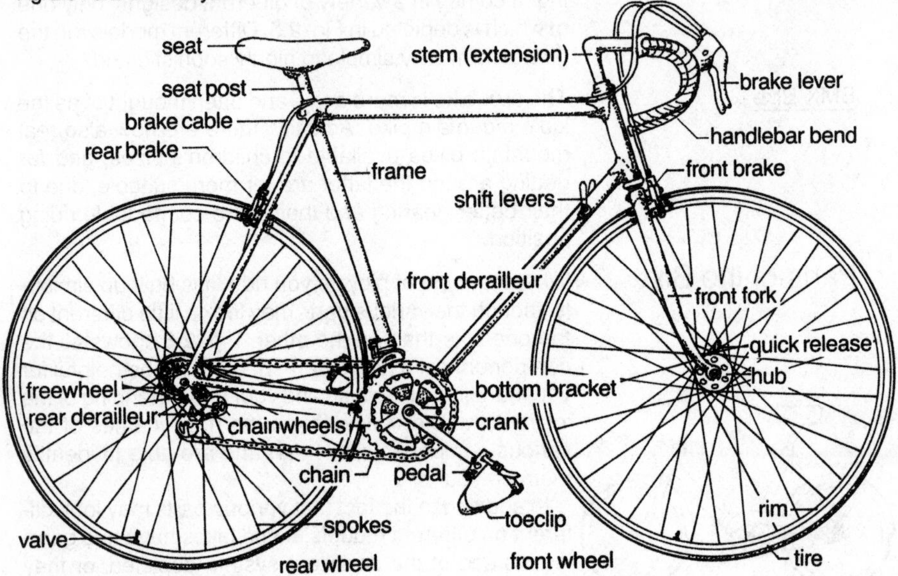

seat

stem (extension)

seat post

brake lever

brake cable

handlebar bend

rear brake

front brake

frame

shift levers

front derailleur

front fork

quick release

hub

freewheel

bottom bracket

rear derailleur

crank

chainwheels

chain

pedal

valve

spokes

toeclip

rim

rear wheel

front wheel

tire

ber of additional accessories, such as fenders (mud guards), racks (carriers) and lights.

The easiest way to memorize the component designations and their names is by considering the various major functional groups of components. The division of maintenance operations in the chapters 5 through 11 follows the same principle. Thus, I shall distinguish the following functional groups, which will each be briefly introduced in the sections that follow.

The Frame

The frame is the bicycle's backbone — the tubular structure to which all the other components are attached. It is made up of steel tubing and comprises the main frame, made up of top tube, seat tube, down tube and head tube, and the rear triangle, made up of parallel pairs of thinner tubes, called chain stays and seat stays, respectively. The rear wheel is installed in the flat plates at the ends of the stays, referred to as dropouts, or (rear) fork-ends.

Maintenance or repair work rarely applies to the frame — and if it should be damaged, chances are that it is too serious to be able to handle it by the roadside. Consequently, this part of the bike is not covered in a chapter of its own.

The Steering System

This system serves both to steer and to balance the bike. It comprises the front fork, the handlebars with its stem, and the headset bearings with which the fork is pivoted in the frame's head tube. The relevant maintenance and repair instructions are covered extensively in Chapter 5.

The Seat

Known as saddle in Britain, this is your major point of contact with the bike. It is held to the frame by means of a seat post, or seat pin. The important adjustments are height and angle, which are covered in Chapter 6, as is tightening both parts.

The Drivetrain

This is the system of components that transmits the rider's effort to the rear wheel. It comprises the crankset (cranks, chainrings and bottom bracket bearings), installed in the frame's lowest point, the bottom bracket; its other components are the chain, the pedals and the freewheel with cogs, or sprockets, on the rear wheel hub. Chapter 7 covers drivetrain maintenance and repair work.

The Gearing System

This is the system that allows matching the transmission ratio to the rider's strength on the one hand, and to the terrain conditions on the other. On most modern bikes it comprises derailleurs with which the chain is shifted from one chainring or sprocket to an other, and the relevant shifters and cables. Some bikes are equipped with a three-speed (or more rarely a five-speed) hub gearing system, built into the rear wheel hub. Both systems will be covered in Chapter 8.

The Wheels

These form the final link between you and the road. Each wheel itself is an assembly comprising a central hub that rotates on ball bearings around a fixed axle, a set of spokes, and a metal rim on which the tire is mounted. Wheel problems are amongst the most common on the bike, and they will be covered extensively in Chapter 9.

The Brakes

The bicycle's brakes are needed to control your speed as well as to stop the bike suddenly at times. Nowadays, virtually all bikes are equipped with some kind of hand brakes that push brake blocks against the sides of the rims. These mechanisms, together with the levers and cables to control them, will be covered in Chapter 10.

Accessories

Different accessories may be present on your bike, or they may be added later. Typical items include a lock, reflectors, lights, luggage racks, fenders, and various other more or less useful embellishments. Chapter 11 gives some suggestions for assuring they remain operational — or at least avoid them becoming a danger.

Chapter 3
Basic Bicycle Tools

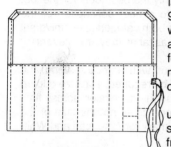

Fig. 3.1 Tool pouch

Selecting Tools

Although it's possible to spend several thousand dollars on bicycle tools and associated equipment, at least 90% of all maintenance and repair work can be done with a very modest outfit. And of those tools, only a few are so essential that they should also be taken along for roadside work. These same tools will suffice for almost all preventive maintenance work, which will be covered in Chapter 4.

The tools discussed here include both regular, or universal, tools that can be bought at any hardware store, and specific bicycle tools that are available only from well stocked bike shops (or some mail order outlets). Buy or sew a pouch (Fig. 3.1) to carry your tools.

Quality counts when buying tools even more than when dealing with other products. Always buy the best tools available, and don't be fooled by terms like 'economy tools', which is merely a polite way of saying 'cheap

Fig. 3.2 Crescent wrench

junk'. Cheap tools don't last and they are less accurate, which makes them harder to work with. After some unsatisfactory use, you'll probably decide to get the better tools anyway, so you finish up spending quite a bit more than you would have done buying the highest quality right away.

Having sworn to buy only the best tools for the job, we can now get down to a brief description of the various essential ones of both categories — universal and special bicycle tools, as far as they are relevant for your basic repair kit.

Note that bicycles are built with metric threading, and thus metric tool sizes will be required. The size quoted in mm (millimeters) will be the dimension across flats of the point where the tool fits — not the size of the screw thread, as is customary for American and Whitworth sizes.

Universal Tools

These are the basic tools that can be purchased in any hardware shop. I will point out which sizes are appropriate for basic repair and maintenance jobs.

Screwdriver

The screwdriver's size is designated by the blade width at the end. You will need a small one with a 4 mm ($^3/_{16}$

in) blade and perhaps a cross-head model if your bike has any screws with cross-shaped recesses instead of the conventional saw cut.

Crescent wrench

This is an adjustable wrench, designated by its overall length. Get a 150 mm (6 in) or a 200 mm (8 in) long model.

Fixed wrenches

Open-ended wrench

Box wrench

Combination wrench

Fig. 3.3 Fixed wrenches

Several different models of fixed wrenches are available, and it will be your choice which you take. You will need sizes from 7 mm to 13 mm.

Box wrenches are the most accurate tools for tightening or loosening nuts and bolts with hexagonal heads. Like all other fixed wrenches, they are designated by the across-flats dimension of the bolt on which they fit, always measured in mm.

Open-ended wrenches are the most common wrenches available. They can be used when there is not enough access room for the box wrench.

Combination wrenches are wrenches that have a box wrench on one end and an open-ended wrench of the same size on the other.

Socket wrenches comprise an L-shaped handle and a set of sockets to fit various size bolts.

Allen keys

Fig. 3.4 Allen key

These hexagonal L-shaped bars, depicted in Fig. 3.4, are used on the screws with hexagonal recesses often used on bicycles. They are designated by the across-flats dimension. Depending on the bolts on your bike, you may need these in the sizes 3.5 mm, 4 mm, 4.5 mm, 5 mm and 6 mm. Occasionally, you may find a use for an even larger model on some bikes.

Pliers

The only model that has a place in your portable repair kit is the needle-nose pliers. But I suggest you don't get tempted to use any one of them whenever another, better fitting tool will do the job, since pliers often do more damage than necessary.

Special Bicycle Tools

The following list of tools made specifically for bicycle use includes only those you will be likely to need in your roadside repair kit.

Pump

This is perhaps your most essential tool. Make sure you get a model that matches the particular valves used on the tubes of your bike (see Chapter 9).

Tire levers

These tools are used to lift the tire off the rim in case of a flat (puncture) or when replacing tube or tire. You need a set of three, and should insist on thin, flat ones that don't bend. For mountain bike tires, which are not as tight-fitting as those used on ten-speeds, there is a special lever that can be used by itself (only one needed), referred to as Zip-stick or quick-stick.

Tire patch kit

Contains most of the other essentials for fixing a flat: patches, rubber solution, sandpaper. This little box also comes in handy to carry some other small spare parts, such as extra nuts and bolts, pump washer, light bulbs

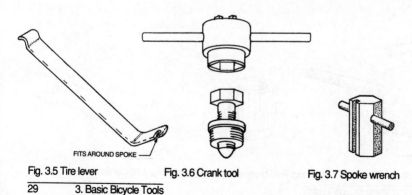

FITS AROUND SPOKE

Fig. 3.5 Tire lever   Fig. 3.6 Crank tool   Fig. 3.7 Spoke wrench

and the like.

Spoke wrench

Called nipple spanner in Britain, this tool is used to tighten, remove or install a spoke, either to replace it or in order to straighten a bent wheel. Make sure you get one that has at least one cut-out in the size that matches the spoke nipples used on your bike.

Crank tool

This tool is needed to tighten or loosen the cranks. Make sure you get a model that matches the particular cranks installed on your bike, since they vary from

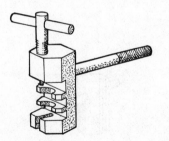

Fig. 3.8 Chain tool

Fig. 3.9 Freewheel tool

Fig. 3.10 Cone wrench

make to make, even from model to model.

Freewheel tool

This item is used to remove a freewheel block from the rear hub, which may be necessary to replace something as basic as a broken spoke. This tool must also be selected to match the particular freewheel used on your bike. If you go to the length of carrying this item, also invest in a so-called pocket vice which allows you to hold it firmly when you have no access to a real vice.

Chain tool

This tool is used to remove a pin that connects the links of the endless chain of a derailleur bike, so it can be

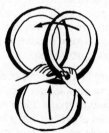

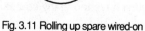

Fig. 3.11 Rolling up spare wired-on

separated for maintenance.

Cone wrenches

These are only relevant for roadside work if you go on a really long tour far away from civilization. These very flat open-ended wrenches are used to overhaul the bearings of a wheel hub. Available in several sizes — it is best to get two of each of the sizes needed for the hubs on your bike.

Additional Items

Depending on the length of the trip, you may want to carry some of the following items: a bottle of water installed on the bike, a tube of waterless hand cleaner, a rag or tissues, and a small first aid kit, including a pair of scissors and a pocket knife, and perhaps some lubricant in a spray can or a well-sealed bottle. Finally, carry a lock, in case you have to leave the bike behind while getting help.

Spare Parts

Here is a list of the spare parts you may find useful to carry on a longer trip. I get by admirably well without many of these. Only twice in 40 years and 200 000 miles of cycling, have I needed a spare tube, but many people seem to feel you can't have too many spares.

My feeling is that adequate preventive maintenance will forestall almost all repairs that require an extensive spare parts inventory.

Spares are no complete substitute for repairs: once you get your second flat, when you have used up that spare tube, you will be confronted with having to fix a puncture anyway. With all that in mind, be guided by your own experience and inclination, aided by the following list:

Brake cable	inner cable only, long enough for rear brake);
Derailleur cable	for rear derailleur;
Spokes	with matching nipples, making sure they are of the right length for both wheels;
Emergency spokes	as described in Chapter 9, to replace broken spokes on the RH side of the rear wheel;
Bolts, washers, and nuts	in 4, 5 and 6 mm sizes;
Rubber seal washer	for pump;
Light bulbs and batteries	for front and rear light, if appropriate;
Inner tube	if you also carry a tire, roll it up per Fig. 3.11.

Chapter 4
Preventive Maintenance

Before proceeding to more detailed instructions, this chapter will help you understand basic procedures and will show you how to keep your bike in good trim, so less is likely to go wrong *en route*. The first part of the chapter will be devoted to the techniques for handling some basic mechanisms found in many places on your bicycle. This includes screw-threaded connections in general, cables and their adjustment, as well as ball bearings and their adjustment and lubrication. The second part of this chapter will be devoted to the procedures to follow for preventive maintenance.

Threaded
Connections

Many of the bicycle's parts are attached, installed and themselves constructed, with threaded connections — not only nuts and bolts, but many other components as well. Essentially, all threaded connections are based on the same principle, shown in Fig. 4.1: a cylindrical, male, part is threaded into a corresponding hollow,

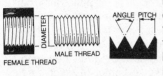

Fig. 4.1 Threaded connection

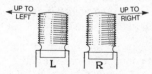

Fig. 4.2 LH and RH thread

female, part by means of matching helical grooves cut into each. When the one part is threaded fully into the other, the reaction force pushes the sides of male and female threads against one another, creating so much friction that the parts are no longer free to turn, thus keeping the connection firm. On the bike, some parts have LH threading, instead of the regular RH thread. LH thread is found on the LH pedal, as well as on a few bearing parts. Fig. 4.2 shows how to tell them apart if they are not marked.

Whether we are talking about a regular nut and bolt or any other threaded part, the way to loosen and tighten the connection is the same. The one part has to be restrained, while the other is turned relative to it — to the right to tighten, the left to loosen in the case of RH thread, the other way round for LH thread. Use exactly fitting tools, to give the best possible hold and to minimize damage. Use tools that offer some leverage (e.g. a wrench with a long handle) on the part that is turned, while the part that is merely restrained may be held with less leverage (e.g. a screwdriver or a shorter wrench).

All threaded connections should be clean and lightly

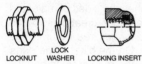

LOCKNUT   LOCK WASHER   LOCKING INSERT

Fig. 4.3 Locking devices

greased when they are installed. If you have difficulty loosening a connection, first squirt some penetrating oil at any accessible point where the male part disappears in the female part. To allow a nut or the head of a bolt to be turned when it is hard down on the part it holds, a plain washer should be installed between the two to reduce friction. This allows you to tighten the joint more firmly.

To minimize the chances of coming loose, e.g. on account of vibrations while riding, many threaded connections are secured one way or another. Fig. 4.3 shows a number of methods used to achieve this: locknut, spring washer and locking insert nut.

If you have problems with parts coming loose, you may use any of these techniques to secure them. A connection that comes loose frequently despite such locking device is probably worn to the point where replacement — usually of both parts — is in order.

Bowden Cables

Brakes and gears on the bicycle are operated via flexible bowden cables that connect the brake or shift lever with the main unit. Fig. 4.4 shows details of a typical cable with end nipple. The inner cable takes up ten-

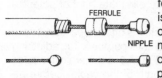

FERRULE

NIPPLE

Fig. 4.4 Bowden cable

sion forces, which are countered by the compression forces taken up by the casing, or outer cable. A nipple is soldered on at one end of the inner cable, while the other end is clamped in at the brake or gear mechanism. Ferrules are installed at the ends of the cable casing to provide a firm termination at the anchor points.

The cables should be kept clean and those for the brakes and those for non-indexed derailleurs should be cleaned and lubricated regularly. The index system invariably uses a stainless steel inner cable with a nylon sleeve between it and the inside of the casing, which makes lubrication unnecessary. By way of lubrication for a regular cable, you may put some vaseline on a rag and run this rag over the inner cable. Once the cable is installed, you may use spraycan lubricant, aiming with the nozzle at the points where the inner cable disappears into the outer casing. Remove excess lubricant with a rag to keep things clean.

When replacing cables, I suggest using stainless steel inner cables, making sure you select them with the same shape nipple used on the original. Some

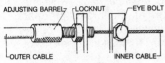

Fig. 4.5 Adjuster detail

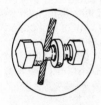

Fig. 4.6 Cable clamp anchor

Quick-Releases

cable casings are available with a low-friction liner of either nylon or PTFE; these eliminate a lot of potential maintenance problems.

Adjusting the cable tension is often necessary to adjust brakes or gears. To this purpose, an adjusting mechanism as shown in Fig. 4.5 is generally installed somewhere along the length of the cable. Before attempting adjustment, make sure the cable end is clamped in firmly. To adjust, loosen the locknut (usually a round knurled design), while restraining the adjusting barrel. Next, unscrew the adjusting barrel far enough to obtain the desired cable tension, and finally tighten the locknut while holding the adjusting barrel to restrain it.

If the length of the adjusting barrel does not allow enough adjusting range, the inner cable must be clamped in further. To do this, first back up the locknut all the way while restraining the adjusting barrel, then screw the adjusting barrel in all the way, and finally clamp the cable in a new location (Fig. 4.6), while keeping it pulled taut with the aid of a pair of pliers.

Quick-release mechanisms are often used on the

wheels, while most ten-speed brake levers and all mountain bike seats also come equipped with some mechanism to loosen and fasten them without tools. The quick-releases for saddle clamp and wheel hubs work on the same principle. Instead of holding the axle or bolt by means of one or two nuts that are screwed down, a toggle lever is used, as shown in Fig. 4.7.

The thumbnut is not intended to be used for tightening the connection, but merely to adjust it in such a way that twisting the lever tightens the whole connection firmly. Open the lever by twisting it, close it by twisting it back. If the connection does not hold, first place the lever in the open position, then tighten the thumbnut perhaps half a turn and try again, until the lever not only holds the part firmly, but can also be opened enough to allow removal or adjustment of the part in question.

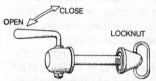

Fig. 4.7 Quick-release

Ball Bearings

Most moving parts run on ball bearings . Their condition has a great effect on the bike's performance. Understanding their operation, maintenance and adjustment is as important for every home bike mechanic as it is for the occasional cyclist who just wants to be sure his bike is operating optimally.

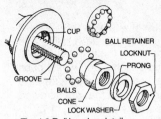

Fig. 4.8 Ball bearing detail

The most common kind of ball bearing in use on the bicycle is the cup-and-cone, or adjustable, bearing shown in Fig. 4.8. These can easily be adjusted and lubricated. Each bearing consists of a cone-shaped and a cup-shaped bearing race, one of which is adjustable relative to the other by means of screw threading. The bearing balls lie in the recess between these two parts and are lubricated to minimize friction. Generally, bearing grease is used as a lubricant. Actually, oil is even more effective, but tends to be messy.

To lubricate with oil, there must be an oil hole in the part. Use relatively thick mineral oil (e.g. SAE 60) in an oil can with a narrow spout. Put a shallow receptacle under the part to be lubricated and fill oil into the oil hole until it comes out at the bearings; allow it to drip a few minutes, then wipe it clean with a rag. Repeat at least once a month and after every ride in very dusty terrain or wet weather.

Grease lubrication only has to be repacked once every one or two years (more frequently if you mainly ride off-road. Either get this job done at a bike shop or follow the instructions in a more comprehensive general bike maintenance book.

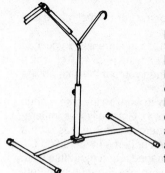

Ball bearings must be so adjusted that the moving part is free to rotate with minimal friction, yet has no 'play' (looseness). To adjust a cup-and-cone bearing, loosen the locknut or lockring while holding the underlying part (the cone in the case of a hub or a pedal, the cup in the case of a headset or bottom bracket). Next, lift the underlying lock washer, if installed, and tighten or loosen the threaded main bearing part (cone or cup) about a quarter of a turn at a time. Finally hold that part again, while tightening the locknut or lockring. Repeat the whole operation if necessary.

Fig. 4.9 Repair stand

Bike Support

When you are out on the road, you can't be too picky, but when doing maintenance work at home, I recommend you use some kind of stand to hold the bike. Several alternatives exist. If you want to splurge, I suggest you get the Blackburn Sporststand or a similar rack (Fig. 4.9). A cheaper alternative is the shop display stand which merely holds the bike and raises the bottom bracket off the ground, so you can balance it with either the rear wheel or the front wheel raised and free to rotate.

Finally, for the devoted do-it-yourselver, you can make a wooden support as shown in Fig. 4.10 on which the handlebars are held when you put the bike upside down.

On the road, the only way to work on the bike is often to place the bike upside down. Generally, it is imperative to support the handlebars about 2 inches off the ground, so the brake cables or items mounted on the handlebars do not get damaged. On a mountain bike, it may suffice to loosen things like the thumb shifters and turn them out of the way temporarily while you work on the bike upside down — just make sure you put them back in the correct position and tighten them afterwards.

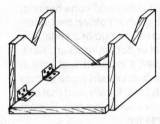

Fig. 4.10 Handlebar support

Preventive Maintenance

At the risk of sounding trite, I must emphasize that in bicycle maintenance an ounce of prevention is worth a pound of repairs. It is actually very simple to keep the bike in good operating condition so it is working well whenever you ride it. That will eliminate the vast majority of necessary repairs later on. It's all a matter

Fig. 4.11 Handlebar check

Daily Inspection

Tires

Handlebars

Saddle

of knowing what to look for and how to put it right before it becomes serious.

Though many of the actual maintenance operations are covered in detail in the chapters that follow, this is the time to get familiar with a systematic schedule to check the bike. It is based on (almost) daily, monthly and annual checks, proceeding as outlined below, referring to the individual chapters that follow to make any corrections that may be necessary.

That may seem to be overdoing it a little, but there are a few things you ought to look out for whenever you take the bike out. These will be covered in this section.

Check whether the tires are inflated properly, i.e. at least as much as is stated on the sidewall, verified with a pressure gauge.

Make sure the handlebars are straight, at the right height and firmly attached. Check while straddling the front wheel and twisting it per Fig. 4.11.

Verify that the saddle is straight and level, at the right height and firmly in place (try twisting it relative to the frame to confirm this).

Brakes	Check the effectiveness of the brakes by verifying that each can block the wheel against your weight, trying to push the bike forward with the lever depressed, leaving about two cm ($^3/_4$ in) between brake lever and handlebars.
Gears	Lift the rear wheel and, while turning the cranks, check whether the derailleurs can be shifted to reach all the gears (every combination of chainring and sprocket).
Monthly Inspection	Do this work at least once a month during the time you use the bike. First clean it as explained below. Then carry out the same inspections listed above for the daily inspection, and do the following additional jobs:
Wheels	Check for broken spokes and wheel wobble: lift the wheel off the ground and turn it relatively slowly, keeping an eye on a fixed point such as the brake blocks. If the wheel seems to wobble sideways relative to the fixed point, it should be trued (see Chapter 9).
Brakes	Observe what happens when you pull the brake levers forcefully: the brake blocks must touch the sides of the rims over their entire surface. Adjust the brakes as outlined in Chapter 10 if they don't.

Tires

Check the tires for external damage and embedded objects. Remove anything that doesn't belong there, and replace the tire if it is badly worn or keeps losing air overnight.

Cranks

Using the crank extractor tool, pull the crank attachment bolts tight, as explained in Chapter 8.

Overall check

Check all the other bolts and nuts on the bike to make sure they are tight. Verify whether all moving parts turn freely and all adjustments are correct. Repair or replace anything damaged or missing.

Lubrication

Lubricate the parts shown in Fig. 4.12, using the lubricants indicated below and wiping any excess off again afterwards:

Chain: special non-gummy chain lube in spraycan;

Brake levers, pivots, cable ends: light spraycan lubricant, aiming precisely with the little tubular nozzle installed on the spray head;

Exposed blank metal parts: vaseline.

Wipe off all excess after lubrication, since exterior grease and oil deposits attract dirt and stain your clothes.

Fig. 4.12 Lubrication points

Annual Inspection

Although most bikes only need this work once a year, You may have to do it more frequently if you ride a lot off-road in bad weather. This is a complete overhauling job, which very nearly returns the bike to its as-bought condition. Proceed as follows:

First carry out all the work described above for the monthly inspection, noting in particular which parts need special attention because they seem to be loose, worn, damaged or missing. Subsequently, work down the following list, getting anything that is necessary carried out at the bike shop (or learn to do it yourself with the help of a general bike maintenance book, such as my *Bicycle Repair Book*).

Wheels

With the wheels still in the bike, check for damage of the rims. Check the hubs for play, wear and tightness as explained in Chapter 9. Preferably disassemble and lubricate or overhaul the hubs.

Chain

Remove the chain and measure the length of a 100 link section — replace the entire chain if it measures more than 51 in (129.5 cm). The apparent stretch is a sign of wear that will affect shifting as well as transmission efficiency. In addition, the worn chain will also wear out the chainrings and the sprockets. If the chain is not badly worn, merely rinse it out in solvent, after which it should be lubricated immediately and reinstalled, following the instructions in Chapter 7.

Bottom Bracket
Check it for play and freedom of rotation. Get it overhauled if it does not run perfectly smoothly.

Headset
Check it as shown in Chapter 5, and if necessary adjust it so it rotates without play or rough spots. If not, get it overhauled.

Derailleurs
With the chain removed, clean, check and lubricate both derailleur mechanisms, making sure the pivots work smoothly and the little wheels or pulleys of the rear derailleur turn freely. If necessary, adjust and overhaul as explained in Chapter 8.

Cleaning the Bike
Do this job whenever your bike gets dirty — preferably at least once a month. It will be much easier to work on a clean bike when something else has to be done. Even this seemingly mundane job requires some thought, proceeding perhaps as follows:

Cleaning procedure:

1. If the bike is dry, wipe it with a soft brush or a rag to remove any dust and other dry dirt. If the bike — or the dirt that adheres to it — is wet, hose or sponge it down with plenty of clean water. Take care not to get the water into the hubs, bottom bracket and headset bearings, though. The same goes for a leather saddle.

2. Using a damp cloth, clean in all the hard-to-get-at nooks and crannies. Wrap the rag around a pointed object, like a screwdriver, to get into hidden places, e.g. between the sprockets on the freewheel and the chainrings, underneath the brake arms, or at the derailleur pulleys.

3. Clean and dry the entire bike with a clean, soft, dry cloth.

4. With a clean vaseline-soaked rag, treat all the blank metal areas very sparingly to inhibit rust.

5. A few times a year, it may be worthwhile to apply car wax to the paintwork.

6. Chrome-plated metal parts may be treated with chrome polish. Anodized aluminum should not be polished (use wax or vaseline instead), since the abrasive polish would remove the protective layer.

Chapter 5
Steering Problems

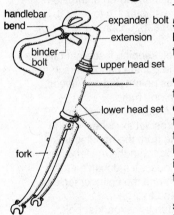

handlebar bend
expander bolt
extension
binder bolt
upper head set
lower head set
fork

Fig. 5.1
Parts of steering system

The parts of the steering system are depicted in Fig. 5.1: front fork, headset bearings, stem and handlebars. We'll cover each of the components, starting at the most frequently necessary jobs.

The handlebars are generally clamped in the stem's clamping collar and the stem is held in the fork's steerer tube, as shown in Fig. 5.2, by means of a wedge- or cone-shaped device. This is pulled into the bottom of the stem with the expander bolt, accessible from the top of the stem and usually equipped with a 6 mm hexagon recess for an allen key. The collar of the stem is generally also equipped with one or more allen bolts to clamp it around the handlebars proper.

Typical maintenance jobs are adjusting and straightening the handlebars. In addition, I shall cover headset bearing adjustment and fork damage, even though the latter can rarely be fixed by the roadside.

Adjust or Tighten Handlebar

Tools and equipment:
Allen key; sometimes a real or improvised hammer and a block of wood for protection

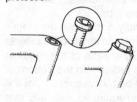

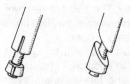

Fig. 5.2 Handlebars and stem

This is required when the bike is set up for a different rider, when the position proves uncomfortable, or when the handlebars are not firmly in place.

Procedure:
1. If the front brake cable is anchored at the stem, first loosen the brake (see Chapter 10) to relax it.
2. If appropriate (i.e. to adjust), unscrew the expander bolt 2—3 turns.
3. Straddle the front wheel, keeping it straight relative to the bike's frame, and put the handlebars in the required position as regards height and orientation, holding it steady there with one hand.
4. If the thing won't turn or move, unscrew the expander bolt two more turns, lift the wheel off the ground, supporting the bike from the handlebars, then tap on the expander bolt with the mallet, after which it will usually come loose. If it doesn't, enter lubricant between the stem and the collar or locknut at the top of the headset and try again.
5. Still holding firmly, tighten the expander bolt.
6. Verify whether the handlebars are now in the right position and make any necessary corrections.

7. If the brake's adjustment was affected (see point 1 above), tension the cable and adjust the brake as outlined in Chapter 10.

Tighten Handlebars in Stem

The connection between the handlebars and the stem should also be firm, so the handlebars don't twist out of their proper orientation. Do this by simply tightening the bolts that clamp the stem collar around the bars.

If the handlebars keep slipping in the stem, lubricate the thread of the binder bolt before tightening it. If this does not do the trick, unscrew the binder bolt fully, wedge the collar open and insert a piece of thin sheet metal (from a discarded beverage can).

Straighten Bent Handlebars

If the handlebars get bent in a fall, it may be possible to bend them back into shape. Only do this if no cracks are apparent at the point where it is bent. Put the bike on its side, the 'good' side of the handlebars down. Hold down the one side and force the other side into shape with all your force. On a mountain bike, remove the handgrips and brake levers and bend with the leverage of a piece of tubing. Don't ride the bike if there are any cracks, and check with the bike shop as soon as possible.

The Headset

Adjust Headset

Tools and equipment:
Special headset wrench or
large crescent wrench

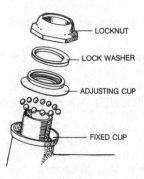

LOCKNUT

LOCK WASHER

ADJUSTING CUP

FIXED CUP

Fig. 5.3 The headset

Shown in Fig. 5.3, this is the set of ball bearings with which the steering system is pivoted in the frame.

When the steering is rough (you will notice resistance when turning the handlebars) or loose (vibrations or clonking noises from the front end), adjust the headset.

Procedure:
1.   Loosen the collar or locknut on the upper headset by one or two turns if there is no serrated ring under it — enough to free the latter if there is.
2.   Lift the washer under this nut enough to release the underlying adjustable bearing cup.
3.   Tighten or loosen the adjustable bearing cup by turning it in the appropriate direction if the bearing is too loose or too tight, respectively.
4.   Put the washer in place and tighten the collar or locknut while holding the adjustable race as well as the fork blades.
5.   Check to make sure the adjustment is correct; readjust if necessary, following the same procedure.

Note:
If adjusting does not solve your problem, the headset

must be overhauled by disassembling it completely, cleaning and lubricating all parts with bearing grease before it is reassembled.

The Front Fork

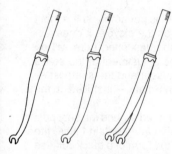

Fig. 5.4 Fork damage

Sometimes, if you hit a pothole or a rock in a fast descent, or when transporting the bike, the front fork may get bent. Fig. 5.4 shows the various kinds of damage possible. Though it will be safest to hitch a ride home if you can, you may be able to straighten some forks. Use a piece of heavy metal tubing (building sites and garages are possible sources) and wedge the bent blade into shape. Inspect the result carefully. Don't ride the bike if cracks are apparent, and always check with the bike shop as soon as possible after any such makeshift repair.

Chapter 6
Seat Problems

Although the seat, or saddle, is not amongst the most trouble-prone components on the bicycle, it does justify some attention. The jobs described here will be limited to basic care and the adjustment of the seat's position. Fig. 6.1 shows the seat and the seatpost — known as seat pin or pillar in Britain — installed on the bike.

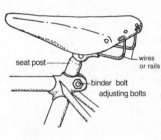

Fig. 6.1
Saddle and seat post

The frame's seat lug is clamped around the seat post by means of the binder bolt. On mountain bikes, the binder bolt invariably takes the form of a quick-release mechanism, which is shown in Fig. 6.3.

The seat height should be adjusted whenever the bike is set up for another rider or when the position is uncomfortably high or low, and tightened when loose.

Adjust Seat Height

In this and the following descriptions, I shall merely explain how the actual adjustment operations are carried out, assuming you know how high you want it.

Tools and equipment:
Wrench to fit binder bolt
(no tools required on
mountain bikes)

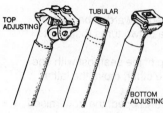

Fig. 6.2 Seat post types

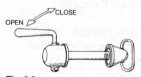

Fig. 6.3
Quick-release binder bolt

Note:

Procedure

1. Undo the binder bolt, or — on the mountain bike — flip the lever of the quick-release in the open position in order to loosen the seatpost.

2. The seatpost with the saddle should now be free to move up and down, if necessary twisting the saddle with the seatpost relative to the frame. If it is not, unscrew the binder bolt (or the QR thumb nut) by about one turn. If it still isn't, enter some liquid lubricant between the seat post and the seat lug, wait a minute or two, and try again.

3. Place the seat in the desired location and hold it there.

4. Holding the seat at the correct height, and aligned perfectly straight forward, tighten the binder bolt — or flip the quick-release lever in the closed position.

5. Check whether the saddle is now installed firmly. If not, repeat the operation.

6. Try out and readjust if necessary until the location is satisfactory.

To ease adjustment, it is a good idea to spread vaseline or other lubricant on the seat post.

Adjust Seat Angle and Position

Tools and equipment:
Allen key or other wrench to fit seatpost adjusting bolts

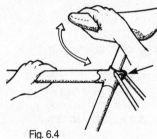

Fig. 6.4
Twist seat to loosen seat post

Generally, both these adjustments are carried out with the same bolt (or bolts) that holds the seat to the seatpost, which can be reached from under the seat.

Procedure:
1. If the seat must be moved forward or backward, loosen the bolt by about one or two turns (both bolts on a two-bolt model).
2. Holding the clamp on top of the seatpost with one hand and the saddle with the other, move the latter in the correct position.
3. If the seat has to be merely tipped, the front raised or lowered relative to the rear portion, loosen the bolt, and then move the saddle in the correct orientation.
4. Holding the seat in the correct location and orientation, tighten the bolt, making sure the seat does not move while doing so.
5. Check and readjust if necessary.

Chapter 7
Drivetrain Problems

The bicycle's drivetrain comprises the parts that transmit the rider's legwork to the rear wheel: the bottom bracket with cranks and chainrings, the pedals, the chain, and the freewheel block with sprockets. The derailleurs, which are sometimes considered part of the drivetrain, will be covered separately in the next chapter, devoted to gearing problems.

The Bottom Bracket

This is the heart of the drivetrain, installed in the frame's bottom bracket shell. It comprises the spindle, or axle, to which the cranks are attached, and the ball bearings that allow it to turn smoothly.

Adjust Bottom Bracket

This job has to be done when the cranks are loose (you'll probably hear clonking noises when pedaling) even though they are themselves attached properly to the bottom bracket spindle, or when the resistance to turning the cranks is excessively high. In the first instance, the bottom bracket bearing has to be tightened; in the latter, it has to be loosened (though lubrication may also be needed in this case)

Tools and equipment:
Provisional tools: blunt narrow screwdriver or pin and hammer

Procedure:
1. Loosen the lockring on the LH side by about one half turn, by hammering the lockring counterclockwise from the slotted recesses in it.
2. Loosen the adjustable bearing cup by turning it by means of the round recesses in the surface of the bearing cup: $^1/_4$ turn counterclockwise if the bearing is too tight, $^1/_4$ turn clockwise if it is too loose.
3. Restraining the bearing cup, tighten the lockring.
4. Check and repeat the adjustment if necessary.

Notes:
1. Of course, it is better to use special bottom bracket tools for this job, but I assume few people carry such tools on a the bike for a roadside repair.
2. Bottom bracket looseness is best detected with the cranks installed, using them for leverage while twisting sideways.
3. Tightness is best established when the cranks are removed, turning the spindle by hand.

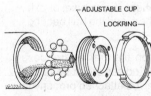

Fig. 7.1
Bottom bracket adjustment

Adjust One-piece Unit

Tools and equipment:
Crescent wrench

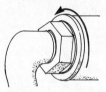

Fig. 7.2
Adjust one-piece unit

The Cranks

To adjust this kind of bottom bracket, which is still used on many American utility bikes and BMX-bikes, proceed as follows:

Procedure:
1.   Countering at one of the cranks, unscrew the big locknut between the LH crank and the bottom bracket by about two turns. It has LH thread, so it is loosened by turning to the right.
2.   Lift the lock washer under the locknut.
3.   Tighten (to the left) or loosen (to the right) the cone that lies under the lock washer.
4.   Seat the lock washer, and retighten the locknut by turning it to the left.
5.   Check operation and repeat if necessary.

Nowadays, most bicycles are equipped with aluminum cotterless cranks. As shown in Fig. 7.3, these are held on square tapered ends of the bottom bracket spindle by a matching square tapered hole and a bolt or nut (depending on the design of the spindle). The bolt or nut is covered by a dustcap, which protects the screw thread in the recess. This screw thread is used to pull the crank off the spindle for maintenance or replacement by means of a crank extractor tool. The RH crank has an attachment spider or flange to which the chainrings are bolted. Low-end bikes sometimes come with either cottered cranks or one-piece cranks.

Tighten Cotterless Crank

<u>Tools and equipment:</u>
Crank tool

The first thing that goes wrong with a new bike with cotterless cranks is usually that the cranks get loose. This is due to the fact that in the beginning the soft aluminum deforms so much that the connection between spindle and crank comes loose frequently until you have covered about 1—200 miles.

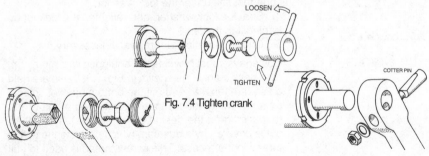

LOOSEN
TIGHTEN

Fig. 7.4 Tighten crank

COTTER PIN

Fig. 7.3 Cotterless crank

Fig. 7.5 Cottered crank

Tighten Cottered Crank

Tools and equipment:
Wrench; real or improvised hammer

If the cotter pin on a cottered crank comes loose, proceed as follows to tighten it:

Procedure:
1. Support the crank at the point where it attaches to the bottom bracket spindle, using a brick or a block of wood resting on the ground.
2. Hammer the cotter pin in further from the side opposite the nut.
3. Tighten the nut firmly.

The Chainrings

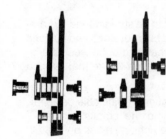

Fig. 7.6 Chainring attachment

The chainrings, or chainwheels, are installed on the RH crank, usually as shown in Fig. 7.6. From time to time, ascertain that the chainrings are still firmly in place by trying to tighten the little bolts that hold them to each other and to the cranks, countering on the other side.

Most chainrings are attached with allen bolts, though some models use slotted nuts on one side, for which a slotted screwdriver or hooked wrench is used. If your front derailleur gives you headaches, one cause may be that the chainrings are either loose or bent, first check and fasten the attachment bolts. If that is not the cause, check just where they are bent by sighting down

Straighten Chainring

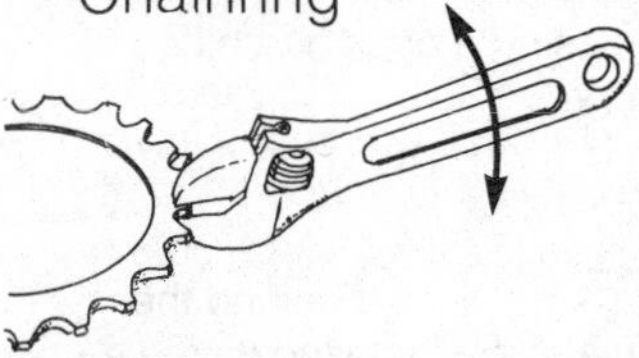

Fig. 7.7
Straighten individual teeth

The Pedals

past the front derailleur while slowly turning the cranks backwards.

If individual teeth are bent, they can sometimes be straightened by grabbing the culprit with a crescent wrench and twisting it back, as shown in Fig. 7.7 (no need to remove the chainwheel from the bike).

If the whole chainring is warped, first establish whether it is an abrupt deformation, or a gradual warp at the location of one of the attachment arms. In the latter case, put a blunt punch against the relevant attachment bolt and strike it firmly with a hammer in the appropriate direction.

If it is an abrupt warp, it can be straightened by carefully using a wedge-shaped block of wood and pushing it between chainstay and chainring or between the individual chainrings in the location where they are too close.

Most pedals run on conventional adjustable ball bearings. They are screwed into the cranks with a RH threaded connection on the right, a LH one on the left. Refer to the Chapter 4 to tell them apart (if not marked).

Replace Pedal

Tools and equipment:
Wrench to fit pedal stub
(sometimes allen key)

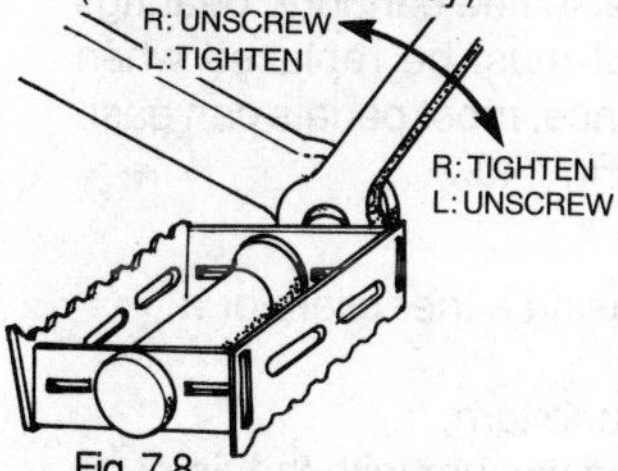

R: UNSCREW
L: TIGHTEN

R: TIGHTEN
L: UNSCREW

Fig. 7.8
Tighten or loosen pedal

Note:

This job may also be necessary to transport the bike, e.g. on a plane, a train or a bus.

Removal procedure:
1. Determine which pedal is the left one: it will have LH thread and must be removed by turning to the right, installed by turning to the left. The RH pedal is loosened to the left, fastened to the right.
2. Unscrew the connection between the pedal and the crank. If the pedal has a hexagonal recess in the end of the threaded stub (reached from behind the crank), use an allen key. If not, use an open-ended wrench.

Installation procedure:
1. Clean the threaded hole in the crank and the threaded stub on the pedal, then apply some vaseline to both threaded surfaces.
2. Carefully align the screw thread and screw in the pedal, turning the RH pedal clockwise, the LH pedal counterclockwise.

If you remove the pedals frequently, e.g. because you often travel with the bike on public transportation, I suggest you place a thin steel washer between the face of the crank and the pedal stub. This will protect the crank and the thread, also making it much easier to loosen and tighten the pedal.

Adjust Pedal

Although some pedals have sealed cartridge bearings that cannot be adjusted but must be replaced when they develop play or resistance, most pedals can easily be adjusted, referring to Fig. 7.9.

Tools and equipment:
Dustcap wrench; wrench to fit locknut; screwdriver

Procedure:
1. Remove the dustcap, using either pliers or a special dustcap wrench.
2. Loosen the locknut by one turn.
3. Lift the underlying keyed washer with the tip of the screwdriver to loosen it.
4. Using the screwdriver, turn the cone to the right (clockwise) to tighten the bearing, to the left (counterclockwise) to loosen it. Turn only $1/4$ turn at a time.
5. Push the keyed washer down and tighten the locknut, restraining the cone so it does not turn.
6. Check and readjust if necessary: there should be neither noticeable play nor tightness.

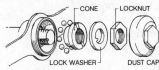

Fig. 7.9
Adjust pedal

7. Reinstall the dust cap.

Bent Pedal Axle

In a fall, the pedal axle may get bent, resulting at a minimum in very irregular, wobbly pedaling, often enough in a pedal that won't turn. To at least ride the bike in the latter case, you may strip the pedal, leaving only the bare axle protruding. Follow the adjusting procedure above, but continue to remove the locknut, the lock washer, and the cone, after which the pedal housing will just come off the axle, spilling the bearing balls all over the place.

The Chain

If you regularly clean, lubricate and replace the chain as described in Chapter 4, the chain will not give you any problems. However, you may have to remove and replace it to carry out other jobs on the bike.

Replace Chain

This has to be done whenever you replace it or remove it for a thorough cleaning job. Also some derailleur maintenance operations are best done with the chain removed from the bike.

Tools and equipment:
Chain tool; rag

Removal procedure:
1. With the aid of the derailleurs, and while turning the cranks with the rear wheel lifted off the ground,

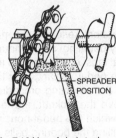

SPREADER POSITION

Fig. 7.10 Use of chain tool

put the chain on the smallest chainring in the front and one of the smallest sprockets in the back.

2. Put the chain tool on one of the pins between two links as shown in Fig. 7.10 with the punch firmed up against it.

3. Turn in the handle by 6 turns, pushing the pin towards the opposite side, and making sure you don't push the pin all the way in — about 0.5 mm (a little more than $1/64$ in) should project on the inside of the link plate.

4. Remove the tool by unscrewing it.

5. Try to separate the chain at this point, twisting it sideways. If it does not work, reinstall the tool and give it another half turn, until the chain comes apart. Just make sure the pin does not come out altogether, since that makes it very hard to reassemble it later.

Installation procedure:

1. Set the derailleurs for the smallest chainring in the front and the second smallest or smallest sprocket in the back.

2. Wrap the chain around chainring, sprocket and

derailleur as shown in Fig. 8.2 in Chapter 8, also passing through the front derailleur cage.

3. Routed this way, there should be just a little spring tension in the rear derailleur, tending to pull it tight.

4. If the chain is too long, remove an *even* number of links, following the same procedure as described above for removal of the chain, but pushing one pin out all the way.

5. Using the chain rivet extractor from the side where the pin protrudes, push it back in until it projects equally far on both sides.

6. Twist the chain sideways a few times until it has come loose enough at this point to bend as freely as at the other links. If this can't be done, put the tool on the chain in the spreader slot (the one closest to the handle) and turn the handle against the pin just a little until the links are freed.

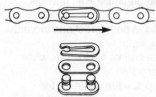

Fig. 7.11 Master link

Note:

The preceding description applies to the removal of the continuous chain for a derailleur bike. The chain for a coaster brake bike or a three-speed has a removable master link, which is used as shown in Fig. 7.11.

Skipping Chain

This is one of the most frustrating problems on the bike, which mainly happens when a gear is selected that engages the smallest sprocket.

Procedure:
1. Turn the cranks backward and watch the chain as it comes off the derailleur tension wheel. If the chain wants to hop up at one particular link, that link should be loosened.
2. Twist the chain sideways in both directions around this link, working it free if possible.
3. Check again, turning the cranks backwards while watching the chain at the sprocket.
4. If the problem persists, place the chain on the chain tool with the stiff pin in the spreader slot (the one nearest the handle).
5. Just barely force the punch of the tool in against the pin, and repeat from the other side until the link is free.

Note:

If this does not solve the problem and the chain has been replaced recently, the freewheel should be replaced as well at the earliest opportunity. Or, if the chain is old, *it* should be replaced (and probably also the smallest sprocket or the entire freewheel block).

Meanwhile, limit the frustration by avoiding the gear that engages the smallest sprocket, because that's usually the only one that gives you this trouble. You can do that by adjusting one of the derailleur's set-stop screws, as explained in Chapter 8.

Replace Freewheel

This job must often be carried out if a spoke on the RH side of the rear wheel has to be replaced. The freewheel and the sprockets also wear, and about once a year it will make sense to replace either the whole freewheel block or the individual sprockets (if it is the casette type that is integrated in the rear hub). In the latter case, refer to the next instruction when replacing sprockets. For roadside repairs, I suggest you purchase a so-called *pocket vice*, a cleverly shaped aluminum casting with which the freewheel tool can be restrained on a railing or other sturdy horizontal metal object.

Tools and equipment:
Freewheel tool; large crescent wrench or pocket vice

Removal procedure:
1.   Remove the rear wheel from the bike, following the instructions in Chapter 9.

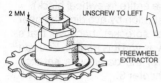

2 MM | UNSCREW TO LEFT

FREEWHEEL EXTRACTOR

Fig. 7.12 Remove freewheel

2. Remove the quick-release or the axle nut and its washer on the RH side.

3. Place the freewheel tool on the freewheel with the ribs or prongs on the tool exactly matching the splines or notches in the freewheel body.

4. Install the quick-release or the RH axle nut, leaving about 2 mm (^{3}/32 in) between tool and nut.

5. If you have a pocket vice available, clamp the tool in with the side matching the freewheel facing up; if not, place the wrench on the flat faces of the tool and clamp the wheel securely, e.g. with the tire pushed against the ground and a wall.

6. Turning counterclockwise to loosen the screw thread between hub and freewheel, forcefully turn either the wheel relative to the vice, or the wrench relative to the wheel — about one turn, until the space between the tool and the nut is taken up.

7. Loosen the nut another turn, and repeat this process until the freewheel can be removed by hand, holding the tool.

Installation procedure

1. Clean the threaded surfaces of the freewheel (inside) and the hub (outside), and coat these surfaces with vaseline to prevent corrosion and to ease future removal.

2. Put the wheel down horizontally with the threaded end facing up.

3. Carefully match the threads, and screw the freewheel on by hand until it cannot be tightened further that way.

4. Install the wheel, and allow the driving force to 'automatically' tighten it as you ride.

Freewheel Problems

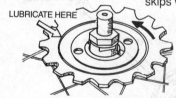

Fig. 7.13 Lubricate freewheel

If the freewheel itself does not work properly, i.e. either the cranks turn whenever the wheel turns or the wheel skips when you pedal, the problem can sometimes be alleviated by removal and subsequent flushing and lubrication with oil: Poor thickish oil in while turning the freewheel, catching the oil in an empty can underneath, until it comes out clean. More often than not, though, it will be necessary to replace the entire freewheel in a case like that.

Chapter 8
Gearing Problems

Virtually all bikes sold these days are equipped with in-dexed derailleur gearing for either 12-, 14-, 18- or 21-speed gearing. Older bikes still use friction shift levers, which are not indexed. That means there are no distinct steps for the individual gears. The derailleurs work

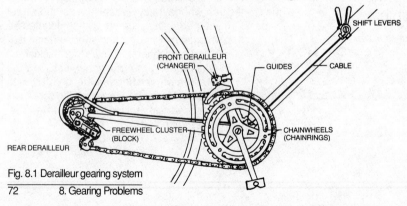

Fig. 8.1 Derailleur gearing system

the same, the only difference lies in the lever, which in its indexed version has a ratchet mechanism with stops corresponding to the individual gears. Most indexed shifters can be set in the friction mode by switching an auxiliary lever or a knob to the F position (the indexed position is marked I). Sometimes, this will be the quick roadside way of making an indexed derailleur work.

Derailleur System

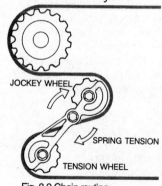

JOCKEY WHEEL

SPRING TENSION

TENSION WHEEL

Fig. 8.2 Chain routing

A typical derailleur system is shown in Fig. 8.1. It consists of a front derailleur, or changer, and a rear derailleur, which are operated by means of shift levers. The shifters may be installed either on the down tube, at the handlebar stem, the bar ends or, in the case of a bike with flat handlebars, on top of the bars (recently also underneath). The shifters are connected to the derailleurs by means of flexible bowden cables.

The derailleurs are used to shift the chain over sideways to engage a smaller or bigger chainwheel or sprocket, while you continue to pedal forward with reduced pedal force. A combination with a large chainwheel and a small sprocket provides a high gear, suitable for easy terrain conditions. Engaging a small chainwheel and a large sprocket provides a low gear, e.g. for hill climbing.

At the rear derailleur, the chain should be routed as shown in Fig. 8.2. This illustration must be consulted whenever you have replaced the wheel, the chain or some other vital part in the drivetrain, until you know by heart how it's done.

Derailleur Care

Before you adjust anything, and in fact also during your monthly maintenance check per Chapter 4, check the following points, which are critical for indexed systems:

a. Keep the derailleurs themselves, as well as the chain and the various sprockets, chainwheels and control cables, clean and lightly lubricated.

b. Adjust the cables so that they are just taut, but not under tension, when the shift lever is in the extreme position, engaging the smallest sprocket or the biggest chainring.

c. Keep the tension screws on the shift levers tightened to give positive shifting when the shifter is set in the F-position.

d. Whenever replacing any part, match it to the make and model of the other gearing components.

Fig. 8.3 Indexed shifter

Adjust Cable Tension

Tools and equipment:
Usually none required;
sometimes wrench and
pliers

This will usually solve the problem when an indexed system does not engage the gears properly. Start out this operation with the shifter in the F-position (assuming an indexed system).

Procedure:
1. Set the derailleur and the chain in the gear corresponding to the released spring tension: always the smallest sprocket in the rear, on most models the smaller chainring in the front.
2. Make sure the shift lever is in the corresponding (released) position.
3. If a cable adjusting device, as shown in Fig. 8.4, is present at the derailleur (always on indexed models), use it to adjust the cable tension: back off the locknut, screw the adjusting barrel in or out as required, and tighten the locknut again, holding the adjusting barrel to stop it from turning with it.
4. If there is no such adjusting mechanism (sometimes the case on non-indexed derailleurs), or if its range is insufficient to solve the problem, loosen the cable clamping bolt on the derailleur, Pull the cable into the clamping bolt to the right location to

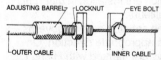
ADJUSTING BARREL LOCKNUT EYE BOLT
OUTER CABLE INNER CABLE
Fig. 8.4 Cable adjustment

keep it just taut, then tighten the bolt again.
5. Check all the gears and readjust if necessary.

Adjust Derailleur

Often one of the derailleurs either pushes the chain too far sideways, off the last chainring or sprocket, or not far enough, so it does not reach the extreme gear. Either problem is solved by adjusting the derailleur's set-stop screws, or limit screws, referring to Fig. 8.5.

<u>Tools and equipment:</u>
Screwdriver

Procedure:
1. Establish where the problem lies:
* Front or rear derailleur?
* Shifted too far or not far enough?
* On the inside or the outside?
2. If necessary, place the chain back on the sprocket or the chainwheel, selecting a gear that combines a small chainring with a small sprocket.
3. Locate the set-stop screws on the particular derailleur mechanism, which are installed in different locations on different derailleurs.
4. Determine which of the set-stop screws governs movement limitation in the appropriate direction. On many models these screws are marked with H and L for high and low gear, respectively. If not, establish

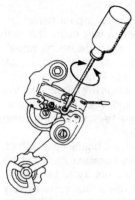

Fig. 8.5 Derailleur adjustment

yourself which is the appropriate screw by observing what happens at the ends of the screws as you shift towards the extreme gears. The high-range set-stop screw is the one towards which an internal protrusion moves as you shift into the highest gear. (On models with neither markings nor visible protrusions, you will have to establish which is which by experimenting.)

5. Unscrew the set-stop screw slightly (perhaps half a turn at a time) to increase the range if the extreme gear could not be reached. Tighten it a little if the chain was shifted beyond that last sprocket.

6. Check all possible gear combinations to establish whether the system works properly now, and fine-tune the adjustment if necessary.

Note:

If the problem can't be solved by the set-stop screw adjustment, it may be due either to a bent derailleur or to incorrect tension on the cable. The former is treated below, the latter can easily be verified by checking whether the cable is taut, but not excessively so, in the extreme gears. If not, follow the instruction *Adjust Cable Tension* above.

Bent Derailleur

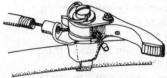

Fig. 8.6 Cable at shifter

Sometimes the problem is due to a bent derailleur, usually caused when the bicycle falls over. The rear derailleur may then be bent inward toward the wheel. This will cause the derailleur to shift too far to the inside and not far enough to the outside. When you try to shift into the lowest gear, the derailleur will rub against the spokes or the spoke guard, and when you try to shift into high gear the derailleur will hesitate shifting down onto the smallest rear sprocket

Establish whether this seems to be the case. Often, what has actually bent is not the derailleur itself, but the RH drop-out, which you should not try to bend back yourself. If you are sure it is the derailleur, you may very carefully try to straighten things out. Let the bike shop check your work when you get home.

Bent or Twisted Front Derailleur

If the front derailleur either does not shift properly or scrapes against the chainring, it may be bent or twisted. Check it by sighting down past the derailleur cage and the chainwheel. If the cage is not perfectly straight, loosen the bolt that clamps the derailleur around the seat tube, and twist the whole thing into the right orientation, then fasten it again.

Replace Broken Cable

Tools and equipment
Wrench; pliers; sometimes vaseline

If you do carry the right spare inner cable, with the appropriate end nipple (check against the one installed at the shift lever), proceed as follows to replace it:

Procedure:
1. Set both derailleurs and the chain in the position with the smallest sprocket and chainwheel.
2. Undo the cable clamping bolt at the derailleur and pull the cable out, pushing the last piece, with the nipple, out at the shifter. Observe over which guides and other parts the cable is routed, so you can replace it correctly later. Catch any loose pieces of outer cable and other parts that may have been used, noting their locations.
3. Lightly apply vaseline all over the new cable to reduce its friction and to prevent corrosion if it is a cable without nylon sleeve.
4. Pull the shift lever over all the way and insert the cable until the nipple is seated in its recess at the shift lever.
5. Route the cable just like the old one was routed and attach it loosely at the derailleur by means of the clamp bolt.

6. If a cable adjusting mechanism is installed, turn it all the way in, following the instructions above.

7. Pull the cable just taut and tighten the cable clamping bolt at the derailleur.

8. Check all the gears, and make any additional adjustments with set-stop screws and cable adjuster that may be required.

9. Cut off the protruding end of the cable to a length of about 3 cm (a little over 1 in), if you have really sharp pliers (otherwise wait until you get to a shop that is appropriately equipped).

Broken Cable / Limit Range

If you don't carry a spare inner cable with you to replace the one that is broken, the rear derailleur will spontaneously shift to the highest gear (smallest sprocket), which may be too high a gear for comfort. In that case, follow the instruction above for adjusting the derailleur, except that you screw in the high-range set-stop screw far enough to limit the range to engage whatever is the highest you can handle continuously.

Adjust Three-Speed

If a three-speed hub does not operate properly, it can also be adjusted quite easily. Before you try to do that, though, make sure the cable runs freely and is not pinched anywhere. Then verify whether all the guides over which it runs are attached to the bike properly, so they don't slip under tension. Refer to Fig. 8.7.

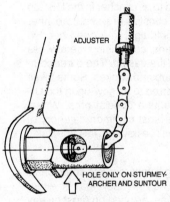

ADJUSTER

HOLE ONLY ON STURMEY-ARCHER AND SUNTOUR

Fig. 8.7
Three-speed adjustment

Procedure:
1.   Set the shift lever in the position for the highest gear (usually marked with number 3 or letter H).
2.   Either pedal back half a revolution or lift the rear wheel off the ground and pedal forward, as will be required for a model with built-in coaster brake. This should engage the appropriate (i.e. highest) gear if the adjustment is correct.
3.   Check the cable tension near the point where it attaches to the operating mechanism at the hub: it must be just taut but not under tension. The slightest movement of the shift lever should also start moving the little chain or the bell crank mechanism to which the cable is attached at the hub.
4.   Use the cable tension adjustment mechanism (following the description for derailleur cable adjustment above if it is of the conventional type, just pushing the spring in on modern types), until the cable tension is correct and each gear engages.

Chapter 9
Wheel Problems

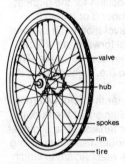

Fig. 9.1 Parts of the wheel

Fig. 9.1 shows a typical bicycle wheel with a regular wired-on tire (often referred to as clincher in the US, tub in Britain). This type of tire consists of a separate inner tube and a cover that is held tight in a deep bedded metal rim by means of beads, comprising metal wires moulded in the side of the tire casing. The other components of the wheel are hub and spokes. Some bikes use a tubular tire, also referred to as sew-up in the US or tub in Britain, which require special rims. Wheel problems are perhaps the most common category of incidents, and their repair will be covered in some detail below.

Remove and Install Wheel

Simple though this is, doing it right requires some basic guidelines which are given here. Wheels may be either installed with a quick-release, as used on most quality bicycles these days, or by means of axle nuts. Refer to Fig. 9.2 and 9.3, respectively.

Tools and equipment:
Wrench (if axle nuts);
rag (if rear wheel)

Fig. 9.2 Axle nuts

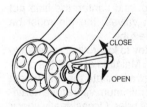

Fig. 9.3 Quick-release

Procedure:
1. On the rear wheel, first place the chain on the smallest sprocket and small chainring with the derailleurs, to minimize tension on the chain.
2. Release tension of the brake, either by means of the brake's quick-release tensioner, by backing off on the adjustment, or by lifting out the cable.
3. On a wheel with axle nuts, undo both by screwing them to the left about three turns. On a wheel with quick-release, move the lever into the 'open' position, and only loosen the thumb nut at the other end if the wheel does not come free otherwise.
4. On a rear wheel, twist back the derailleur and the chain as shown in Fig. 9.4.
5. Raise the bike (unless it's held upside-down), and remove the wheel.
6. To install, proceed in reverse order, making sure you place the washers of a wheel with axle nuts between the nut and the fork-ends or drop-outs, and holding back the rear derailleur to allow the sprocket to return to its proper position and the chain to wrap around it as shown in Fig. 8.2 in Chapter 8.
7. Hold the wheel exactly aligned in the center

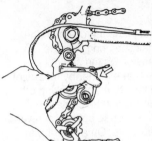

Fig. 9.4 Hold back derailleur

Tires and Tubes

between the fork blades or stays. Tighten the axle nuts, each time countering at the other one, or tension the quick-release by putting the lever in the 'closed' position — after retightening the thumb nut if you should have loosened it under point 3 above.

8. Retension the brake, and make any other adjustments that may be necessary. Sometimes, if the brakes are too tight, you have to let the air out of the tire — that should be a last resort, after which it should be inflated properly again.

The tube is inflated by means of a valve, several types of which are illustrated in Fig. 9.5. On the Presta valve, first unscrew the round nut at the tip, and push the pin in to free it, before inflating, and tighten the little nut again afterwards. On both valves, the pin must be pushed in to let air out of the tube

Inflation pressure is the key to low rolling resistance and immunity to puncturing. Maintain at least the pressure quoted on the tire sidewall. Inflate the rear wheel by up to 20% more than that minimum value for a heavily loaded bike, less for a light rider. Occasionally check the pressure with the aid of a tire pressure gauge.

Presta   Schrader

Fig. 9.5 Valve types

Fixing a Flat

The flat, or puncture, is probably the most frequently encountered bike problem. It really is a very simple repair, that will be outlined below for the regular wired-on tire. Some people suggest replacing the tube, but you can't carry unlimited spares, and you may get more than one puncture a day.

<u>Tools and equipment:</u>
Patch kit; tire levers; pump (and tools to remove wheel)

<u>Procedure:</u>
1. Remove the wheel from the bike. Follow the appropriate instructions above for wheel removal.
2. Check whether the cause is visible from the outside. In that case, remove it and mark its location, so you know where to work.
3. Remove the valve cap and the locknut, unscrew the round nut (if you have a Presta valve).
4. Push the valve body in and work one side of the tire into the deeper center of the rim, as shown in Fig. 9.6.
5. Put a tire lever under the bead on the side that has been freed, at some distance from the valve, then use it to lift the bead over the rim edge and hook it on a spoke, as shown in Fig. 9.7.
6. Do the same with the second tire lever two spokes

Fig. 9.6 Push sidewall in

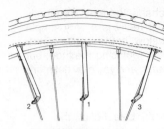

Fig. 9.7 Install tire levers

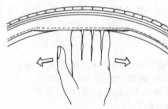

Fig. 9.8 Work tire off by hand

to the left, and with the third one two spokes over to the right. Now the first tire lever will come loose, so you may use it in a fourth location, if necessary.

7. When enough of the tire sidewall is lifted over the rim, you can remove the rest by hand (Fig. 9.8).

8. Remove the tube, saving the valve until last. Push the valve out through the valve hole in the rim, while holding back the tire.

9. Try inflating the tire, and check where air escapes. If the hole is very small, so it can't be easily detected, pass the tube slowly past your eye, which is quite sensitive. If you have difficulty finding the hole, and if you have access to enough water, dip the tube under water, a section at a time: the hole is wherever bubbles escape. There may be more than just one hole.

10. Make sure the area around the hole is dry and clean, then roughen it with the sand paper or the scraper from the patch kit, and remove the resulting dust. Treat an area slightly larger than the patch you want to use.

11. Quickly and evenly, spread a thin film of rubber solution on the treated area. Let dry about 3 minutes

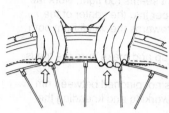

Fig. 9.9 Install tire by hand

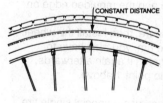

CONSTANT DISTANCE

Fig. 9.10 Center tire

in hot, dry weather, up to twice as long in cold or humid weather.

12. Remove the foil backing from the patch, without touching the adhesive side. Place it with the adhesive side down on the treated area, centered on the hole. Apply pressure over the entire patch to improve adhesion.

13. Sprinkle talcum powder from the patch kit over the treated area, or you can leave the cellophane on the patch so it does not stick to the inside of the tire.

14. Inflate the tube and wait long enough to make sure the repair is carried out properly.

15. Meanwhile, check the inside of the tire casing, and remove any sharp objects that may have caused the puncture.

16. Let enough air out of the tube to make it limp but not completely empty.

17. Push the tire far enough on the rim to allow seating the tube completely in the rim bed under the tire, starting by putting the valve through the hole in the rim.

18. *With your bare hands*, pull the tire back over the edge of the rim (Fig. 9.9), starting opposite the valve, which is best last of all. If it seems too tight, work the part already installed deeper into the center of the rim bed, working around towards the valve from both sides.

19. Push the valve stem up and make sure the tire is fully seated.

20. Make sure the tube is not pinched between rim and tire bead anywhere, working and kneading the tire until it is free.

21. Install the valve locknut, if appropriate for the type of valve used, and inflate the tire to about a third its final pressure.

22. Center the tire relative to the rim, making sure it lies evenly all around on both sides, checking the distance between the rim and the moulded ridge on the side (Fig. 9.10).

23 Inflate to its final pressure, then install the wheel. If the tire is wider than the rim, you may have to release the brake, and tighten it again afterwards. On the rear wheel, refer to point 1 above.

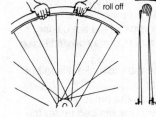

roll off

Fig. 9.11 Roll off tubular tire

Note:

Instead of steps 5—7, if you use a special single tire lever (*Zipstick* or *Quickstick*), insert it with the grooved side up, then twist it towards the spokes and follow the tire around the wheel, pulling more and more off the rim as you work your way around.

Replace Tube or Tire

Although I have rarely found it necessary, most people always carry a spare tube and replace the entire thing, rather than repairing the old tube. This must also be done if the valve leaks or if the tube is seriously damaged. It is done following the relevant steps of the instructions for fixing a flat. Replacement of the tire casing is done similarly. Make sure the rim tape that covers the spoke ends is intact (join the ends with a patch if necessary).

Replace Tubular Tire

That's about all you can do by the roadside if you have a problem with a tubular tire. One good reason not to use these highly sensitive and rather expensive goodies. Consider equipping your bike with wheels for wired-on tires if you have frequent flats or other problems with your tubulars. To replace a defective tubular tire, first remove the wheel from the bike, as explained in a previous section of this chapter. Carry only used tubulars that have adhesive on as spares, since these stay in place better and are easier to put on.

Fig. 9.12 Stretch tubular tire

Removal procedure:

1. Remove the cap from the valve, then unscrew the valve and push the pin in to let any remaining air out.

2. If there is a locknut on the valve (there should not be), remove and discard it.

3. Starting opposite the valve, push off the tire, rolling it off by hand pressure, working your way around gently in both directions towards the valve, as shown in Fig. 9.11.

4. When the tire is off over its entire circumference, take the valve out of the valve hole in the rim.

Installation procedure:

1. If it does not seem to fit, first stretch it, pulling it between feet and hands, as shown in Fig. 9.12.

2. Inflate the tire just enough so it does not hang limp, without putting pressure on it.

3. Place the valve through the valve hole in the rim, and pull the tire around the circumference of the rim, working around both ways, applying enough force to keep it stretched.

4. Once the entire tire is on the rim, straighten it out, so the black tread portion is perfectly centered with respect to the rim.

The adhesive with which the tire is held to the rim is effective enough to hold a replacement tire, providing you don't ride around sharp curves too vigorously. Once you get home, take the thing down and apply new adhesive to the rim bed, installing the tire after it has become tacky. Repair the old tire (or have it done for you by a professional), so you can take it as a spare on your next ride.

Adjust Hub Bearings

If the wheel is loose or does not turn freely, although everything else is OK, the wheel bearing may have to be adjusted, referring to Fig. 9.13. If it is very loose and adjusting does not help, the axle may be broken. If that is the case, you may carefully ride a bike with a quick-release hub, but don't ride the type with axle nuts since there is nothing to keep the parts together on that model. Either way, try to get to a bike shop to have the repair carried out as soon as possible.

To adjust a wheel with axle nuts, just remove the nut on one side (choose the LH side if it is the rear hub), leaving the other nut tightened. A wheel with a quick-release hub should be removed from the bike.

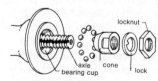

Fig. 9.13 Bearing detail

Tools and equipment:
Crescent wrench; cone wrench

Procedure:
1. Loosen the locknut (on the loosened side in case the wheel remains in the bike) by about two turns, countering at the underlying cone with the cone wrench.
2. Lift up the lock washer to free the cone.
3. Tighten or loosen the locknut by screwing it to the right or the left, respectively, countering from the opposite locknut or cone in case the wheel was removed from the bike.
4. Retighten the locknut, countering at the cone that was just adjusted.
5. Check operation of the wheel, and readjust if necessary.

The Spokes

The spokes, shown in Fig. 9.14, hold hub and rim together into a stressed unit. Each spoke is held to the rim by means of a screwed-on nipple. It should be kept tightened to maintain the spoke under tension, which actually prevents a lot of spoke breakages. The spokes run from the hub to the rim in one of several distinct patterns. Fig. 9.15 shows three-cross and four-cross spoking patterns — check which is used on your bike.

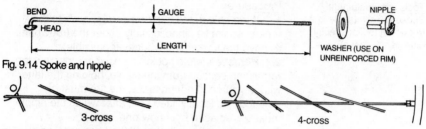

Fig. 9.14 Spoke and nipple

Fig. 9.15 Three-cross and four cross spoking patterns

If a spoke should break, carry out a repair according to the following description.

Replace Broken Spoke

You're in luck if it is a spoke on the front wheel or the LH side of the rear wheel, since those are adequately accessible at the hub. On the RH side of the rear wheel, on the other hand, the spoke hole in the hub is hidden by the freewheel with its sprockets. If you have a free-wheel that can easily be removed — or one that allows the sprockets to be removed easily — do so and follow the instructions below, which apply to accessible spokes. If not, see the remark at the end of these instructions.

Tools and equipment:
Spoke wrench (sometimes freewheel tool or special emergency spoke)

Procedure:
1. If the hole in the hub that corresponds to the broken spoke lies inaccessibly under the freewheel, remove the freewheel (whenever possible).
2. Remove the old spoke. If possible, unscrew the remaining section from the nipple, holding the latter with a wrench. If not possible, the tire must be deflated and locally lifted first, after which the nipple must be replaced by a new one.
3. Locate a spoke that runs the same way as the broken one: every fourth spoke along the circumference of the rim runs similarly. Check how it crosses the various other spokes that run the other way, using it as an example.
4. Thread the nipple on the spoke until the latter has the same tension as the other spokes of the wheel.
5. If the spokes do not seem to be under tension, tighten all of them half a turn at a time, until they all seem equally taut and the wheel is reasonably true. If necessary, follow the instructions for *Wheel Truing* below to correct the situation.

Note:

You can replace an inaccessible spoke by a

Fig. 9.16 Emergency spoke

BEND AS SHOWN

detail

temporary one. Do that by bending an overlong spoke into the shape shown in Fig. 9.16, which allows you to hook it in from between the freewheel sprocket and the hub flange. It will break if you have to bend and rebend it several times before you have established the right size — so it is best to make up some spokes of the correct size at home before you leave. Replace it by a 'real' spoke upon your return.

The Rims

One problem that may happen to you when touring, usually in combination with spoke breakage, is a seriously bent wheel. It will wobble sideways and rub against the brake or other parts of the bike intermittently. Before doing anything about the rim, replace any broken spokes.

A small local dent, usually the result of riding over a sharp protrusion with inadequately inflated tires, can sometimes be relieved provisionally: remove the wheel and place the rim with the 'good' side on a firm, level surface. Hammer the dent out from the other side. Get the job done properly at the bike shop when you return home — usually by replacing the entire rim.

Wheel Truing

If the problem is more serious one, the wheel being bent quite far over a larger area, first straighten the thing roughly. Do that with the wheel removed from the bike. Support it in its two 'low' points, e.g. against the pavement and the curb, while pushing against it in the 'high' points, as shown in Fig. 9.17. Push and check and push again, until the thing begins to look like it is level, and none of the spokes seem to be excessively loose. Then proceed to the truing operation outlined below.

Tools and equipment
Spoke wrench

Procedure

1. Check just where it is offset to the left, where to the right, by turning it slowly while watching at a fixed reference point, such as the brake shoes. Mark the relevant sections.
2. Tighten LH spokes in the area where the rim is off-set to the RH side, while loosening the ones on the LH side — and vice versa, as shown in Fig. 9.18.
3. Repeat steps 1 and 2 several times, until the

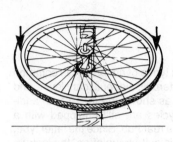

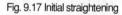

Fig. 9.17 Initial straightening

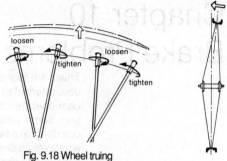

Fig. 9.18 Wheel truing

wheel is true enough not to rub on the brakes.

Note: As so many other emergency repairs, this is not a permanent rectification of a serious problem. It will get you by, but you should get the job checked and, if necessary, done properly by a mechanic at the bike shop as soon as possible.

Chapter 10
Brake Problems

There are four different types of rim brakes in common use, referred to as centerpull, sidepull, cantilever, and cam-operated brakes, as shown in Fig. 10.1. In addition, some simple bicycles are still equipped with a coaster brake built in the rear hub. Since the latter type, whatever its demerits, is quite troublefree, the instructions in this chapter will deal primarily with the adjustment and repair operations for the various kinds of rim brakes.

Compare the brakes used on your bike with those shown in the illustration, to verify which type is used. On the sidepull brake, the brake arms pivot around the attachment bolt, while they pivot around separate bosses installed on a common yoke on the centerpull brake and on the removable version of the cam-operated brake. On the cantilever brake and the frame-mounted varieties of the centerpull and cam-operated models,

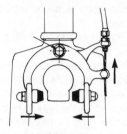

Sidepull brake

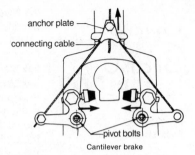

anchor plate

connecting cable

pivot bolts

Cantilever brake

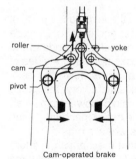

roller

yoke

cam

pivot

Cam-operated brake

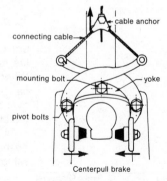

cable anchor

connecting cable

mounting bolt

yoke

pivot bolts

Centerpull brake

Fig. 10.1 Brake Types

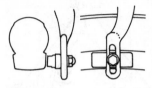

Fig. 10.2
Brake block alignment

the pivots are installed on bosses that are attached directly to the fork or the stays.

With any rim brake, the force applied by pulling the lever is transmitted to the brake unit by means of flexible cables. These cables are partly contained in flexible outer cables and restrained at anchor points on the frame. On ten-speeds, a quick-release mechanism is usually built in somewhere along the way to release the cable tension, so the wheel may be removed past the brake, and to ease work like replacing or adjusting the cable.

The force is transmitted from the lever to the parts of the brake unit to which the inner and outer cables are attached. A pivoting action then pulls the ends of the brake arms with the brake blocks against the sides of the rim to create the drag that slows down the bike. When the brake does not work satisfactory, the cause can be in any element of the chain of power from lever, over cable and anchors, via the brake mechanism and the brake blocks to the bicycle wheel's rim.

All brakes have an adjustment mechanism to shorten the cable, which allows you to apply sufficient force without the thing bottoming out. It may be installed at the lever, at the brake unit, or at one of the cable anchor points. The adjustment is described below. Brake cables should not be elastic, or 'spungy', to allow applying adequate force. They should be routed as short as possible, without forcing them in excessively tight bends in any position of handlebars or brake.

Brake Check

To make sure the brakes work properly, it is enough to test them at low speed. Try them out separately at walking speed, which is perfectly safe and still gives a representative test of the deceleration reached with each brake. Used singly while riding the bike at walking speed, the rear brake must be strong enough to skid the wheel when the lever is applied firmly. The front brake should decelerate the bike so much that the rider notices the rear wheel lifting off when it is fully applied. If their performance is inadequate, carry out the adjustment described below.

Fig. 10.3
Mountain bike brake adjuster

Adjust Brake

We will assume the brake must be adjusted because its performance is insufficient. In this case, the tension must be increased by decreasing the inner cable's effective length. Should the brake touch the rim even

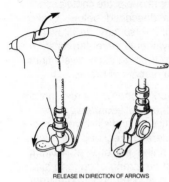

RELEASE IN DIRECTION OF ARROWS

Fig. 10.4 Brake quick-releases

Tools and equipment:
Usually none required

when not engaged, the opposite must be done to lengthen the inner cable. The adjuster mechanism is described in Chapter 4. Mountain bikes have an adjuster built in the lever, as shown in Fig. 10.3.

Before starting, check to make sure the brake blocks lie on the rim properly over their entire width and length when the brake is applied, as shown in Fig. 10.2. Ideally, the front of the brake block should touch the rim just a little earlier than the back. If necessary, adjust by loosening the brake block bolt; move the brake block as appropriate, and then retighten it while holding it in the right position. If necessary, the brake block may be replaced when you get to a bike shop, after which the adjustment steps that follow must be carried out as well.

Procedure:
1.   Release the brake quick-release, as shown in Fig. 10.4, if installed (or release the transverse cable on cantilever and U-brakes, the cam on cam-operated models).
2.   Loosen the locknut on the adjusting mechanism for the brake cable.

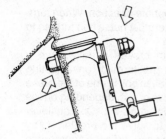

Fig. 10.5 Center sidepull brake

Center Brake

Fig. 10.6
Inner cable and nipples

3. While holding the locknut, screw the barrel adjuster out by several turns; then tighten the quick-release again.

4. Check the brake tension: the brake must grab the rim firmly when a minimum of 2 cm (^{3}/4 in) clearance remains between the brake lever and the handlebars.

5. If necessary, repeat steps 1—4 until the brake works properly.

6. Tighten the locknut again, while holding the adjusting barrel to stop it from turning.

If the rim brake rubs on one side of the rim, even though the wheel is adjusted correctly and the problem remains after adjusting the brake, it should be centered. On a centerpull brake, put a punch or a screwdriver on the side of the yoke that is too high, and tap it down with a real or improvised hammer.

To center a sidepull brake, most manufacturers provide special tools, usually in the form of a thin wrench to twist the pivot and mounting bolt. If no special tool is available, twist the mounting bolt by simultaneously turning the nut in the rear of the brake attachment and one of the two nuts on top of the brake (see Fig. 10.5) in the appropriate direction: When turning to the right, pick the outermost nut; when turning to the left the one underneath.

U-brakes and roller-cam brakes usually have a centering aid provided in the form of an adjusting screw. This is usually a tiny allen bolt in one of the brake arms that must be screwed in or out, depending on the direction in which the brake is off-set. On cantilever brakes, the usual method to solve the problem is by bending the brake arm return springs in the appropriate direction with needle-nose pliers.

Brake System Repair

Tools and equipment:
Wrench; pliers; lubricant

If the brake cannot be made to operate properly, despite all efforts to adjust, the problem may be caused by excessive friction or looseness in one of the mechanical elements. Proceed as follows.

Procedure:
1. Check whether all attachment bolts are tightened and none of the parts are either bent or otherwise inoperative.
2. Push the brake blocks against the rim by pushing in the brake arms and let them come back. If they can't be pushed together or don't return under the

Fig. 10.7
Broken cable strands

spring's force alone, the brake mechanism itself is at fault. Use oil at the pivots, try to free the individual pivot points, and straighten any parts that are bent and rub against one another.

3. If the problem persists, proceed to the cable. Loosen or unhook the cable at the brake mechanism, then check whether the inner cable is free to move relative to the outer cable. If not, try lubricating the inner cable at all points where it enters the outer cable or runs through or over guiding parts. If that doesn't help, disassemble the cable and use the pliers to work on any protrusions on the outer cable on which the inner cable may have hung up.

4. If this does not do the trick, try out the lever. If it does not operate freely, try lubricating the pivot, loosening or tightening the pivot bolts, straightening any deformed parts that may present friction.

5. Scrape or roughen the brake block surface, e.g with steel wool, especially if the brake squeals.

6. Finally, reassemble everything, making sure all connections are tight, all pivots are free to move, and there are no kinks in the cable. If necessary, readjust the brake as described before.

Replace Brake Cable

To avoid the unsettling experience of the brake cable snapping just when it is most needed, replace it as soon as individual strands show signs of damage at the end nipple, as shown in Fig. 10.7. Make sure the replacement cable has a nipple that matches the particular brake lever used on your bike.

Tools and equipment:
Wrench; pliers; if available, third hand tool

Procedure:
1. Loosen the brake quick-release. On a U-brake or a cantilever brake, push the brake arms together and take out one of the nipples of the connecting straddle cable. On a frame-mounted cam-operated brake, push the brake arms together and twist out the cam plate.
2. Loosen the clamp or eye bolt that holds the cable at the brake, until you can free the old cable.
3. Push the old cable out, working towards the lever, where you can dislodge the nipple as shown in Fig. 10.8. On a mountain bike brake lever (Fig. 10.3), turn the adjuster into such a position that the slot in the lever is free, so you can take out the cable.

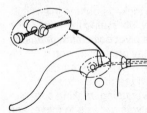

Fig. 10.8 Nipple in lever

4. Pull the entire inner cable out, catching the outer

cable section or sections, as well as any other parts, memorizing their installation locations.

5. Lubricate the new cable. Back off on the locknut, then screw the adjusting barrel in all the way.

6. Starting at the lever, push the new cable through, securing the nipple by pulling it taut. Thread the cable through the adjuster, the various anchor points, outer cable sections and other parts.

7. Push the brake blocks with the brake arms against the rim, preferably using the third hand brake tool illustrated in Fig. 10.9.

8. Push the cable end through the eye bolt at the brake, and tighten the bolt hand-tight. Secure the nipple into the lever by pulling the cable taut from the brake end.

9. Tighten the eye bolt while continuing to keep the cable taut.

10. Adjust the cable tension, following the preceding instructions.

11. Test the brake in operation. Pull the lever forcefully, holding it several minutes to stretch the cable, followed by a final adjustment if necessary.

12. Finally, cut off the free end of cable until about

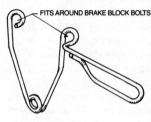

FITS AROUND BRAKE BLOCK BOLTS

Fig. 10.9 Third hand tool

3 cm ($1\frac{1}{4}$ in) projects, using sharp cutters. Wait until you get to a bike shop or garage to do that if you don't have the right tool.

Coaster Brake Problems

If you ride a bike with a coaster brake, the worst that can happen is that your chain breaks or that the counter lever on the LH side that holds the inner life of the brake fixed to the bike's frame comes loose.

If the chain snaps, you will not be able to brake at all, and will have to steer towards a likely place to come to a standstill without serious harm to body and bike. Use spare chain links and the chain tool to mend the chain, roughly following the instructions for chain assembly in Chapter 7. If you don't have spare chain links, you may be able to shorten the chain slightly and compensate for it by pushing the wheel further forward, not forgetting to loosen and subsequently tighten the attachment of the lever on the LH side of the hub.

If the lever comes loose, you will notice unreliable and intermittent operation, both when braking and when accelerating subsequently. Pull the lever back in the correct position, and use a spare bolt to attach it firmly to the clamp around the LH chain stay.

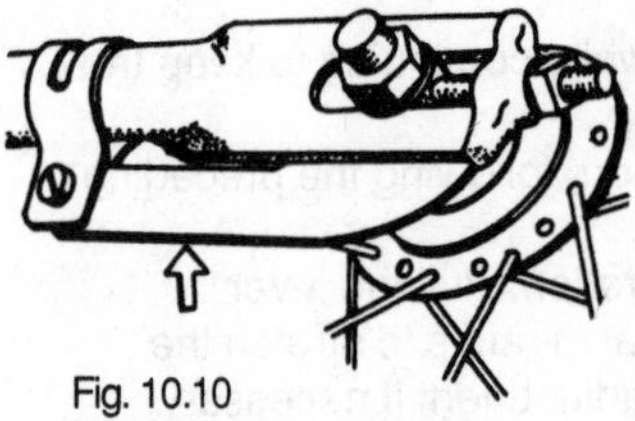

Fig. 10.10
Coaster brake counter lever

Chapter 11
Accessory Problems

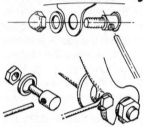

Fig. 11.1 Fender attachment

The one advantage of many accessories from a maintenance standpoint is probably the fact that they are not essential. Consequently, they can be removed and perhaps even discarded when they cause you grief along the way. As for the (under certain circumstances) essential accessories, such as lights and luggage racks, attaching them properly, and perhaps replacing their attachment hardware, is the most important advice. It will be helpful if you carry some spare bolts, washers and nuts in your tire patch kit for such purposes.

Fenders

If the fenders or the stays with which they are attached rub against the wheels, don't just bend the stays like wishbones to relieve the problem. Instead, loosen the attachment bolts, shown in Fig. 11.1, straighten anything that is bent, and slide the stays in such a position that the whole affair is in order, before tightening the attachment bolts. In order to stop the bolts from loosening, you may apply Locktite thread sealer to all screw threads before screwing the nuts on.

Pump

Though more properly a tool, we'll cover the pump as an accessory here. If the thing doesn't do its job, first see whether it helps to tighten the screw-on cap at the head, where you place it on the valve. If still no luck, unscrew it and turn over and massage the thick rubber washer that lies inside, after which the cap is screwed on firmly again. Finally, you may remove the plunger from the other end of the pump barrel (see Fig. 11.2) and try greasing and kneading it. In arid climates, grease the plunger twice a year.

Lock

If your lock doesn't work, lubrication often does the trick. Don't just pour oil (from a supposedly empty can at any gas station, if you don't carry your own) down

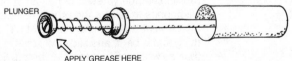

PLUNGER

APPLY GREASE HERE

Fig. 11.2 Pump maintenance

Generator lighting check

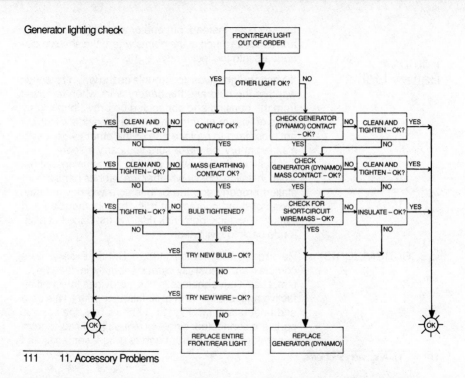

the key hole. Instead, put one or two drops on the key and about as much at the points where the shackle disappears into the lock body.

Battery Lights

If a battery light gives you trouble on the way, first check whether the bulb and the battery work when removed from the housing and connected up provisionally (any piece of wire or metal found by the roadside will do). If not, you have to replace one or the other — generally it's the battery, so make sure you carry a spare.

If bulb and battery work outside the housing, but not when installed, check whether the various parts are installed properly and the bulb is screwed down firmly. Clean or bend contacts of bulb, battery, housing and switch. If no luck, don't risk riding in the dark, but hitch a ride back to civilization.

Generator Lights

Referred to as dynamo lighting in Britain, this is a more complex and generally rather shoddily installed system. I use it nevertheless, since it provides the most effective and reliable form of illumination with a little care and understanding. Fig. 11.3 shows how the various parts are connected: single-pole insulated cables from generator contact to front and rear light contacts, and

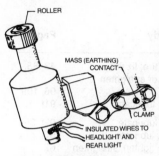

ROLLER

MASS (EARTHING) CONTACT

CLAMP

INSULATED WIRES TO HEADLIGHT AND REAR LIGHT

Fig. 11.4 Generator detail

bare metal connections between the various parts and the frame for the other electric pole.

If the thing gives you trouble, first check whether the roller actually contacts the tire and the centerline through the unit is aligned towards the center of the wheel. If that is correct, start searching the fault systematically, being guided by the simplified logic diagram Fig. 11.3, also referring to Fig. 11.4 to establish which connection is which. In your supply of spare parts, make sure you at least have one of each of the bulbs required and preferably about 8 ft of insulated wire. That will be sufficient to solve at least 90% of your lighting problems.

Troubleshooting Guide

Problem/symptom	Cause	Remedy	Page
High resistance (pedaling and coasting)	1. insufficient tire pressure	inflate tire, fix flat	43, 85
	2. tire rubs on frame or accessory	adjust or straighten	96, 109
	3. wheel bearing problems	adjust, lubricate	91f
High resistance (pedaling only)	1. chain dirty, dry, worn	clean, lubricate	92f, 96
	2. bottom bracket problems	adjust, lubricate	57f
	3. chainring rubs on frame	adjust, tighten, straighten	62
Bike pulls to one side	1. wheel misaligned	adjust, center, straighten	82f, 96
	2. front fork bent	straighten	53
Bike vibrates	1. wheels not true	true (straighten) wheel	96
	2. headset loose	adjust headset	52
	3. hub axle or bearings loose	tighten, adjust	82f, 91
Chain skips off sprocket	1. stiff or damaged chain link,	free link by twisting	67f
	2. clean, lubricate, fasten, sprocket worn	limit derailleur range (later replace)	76
	3. chain worn or damaged	adjust, lubricate, replace	43, 65f

Problem/symptom	Cause	Remedy	Page
Chain drops off chainring or sprocket when shifting	1. derailleur out of adjustment	adjust derailleur	76
	2. derailleur or drop-out bent	straighten	78
	3. chainring loose or bent	tighten or straighten	61f
	4. chain loose	shorten chain or move wheel back	65f, 82f
Irregular pedaling motion	1. crank, bottom bracket or pedal loose	tighten or adjust	60f, 57f, 64
	2. crank or pedal axle bent	straighten or replace (or strip pedal)	65
Gears do not engage properly	1. derailleur or hub-gear problems	clean, adjust, fasten or free	74f, 80
	2. gear control problems	clean, lubricate, fasten, free, replace	74f
	3. chain too loose, tight or worn	correct chain length	65f
Rim brake jitters	1. rim damaged	straighten or replace	95f
	2. brake loose	adjust and tighten brake	104
	3. headset loose	adjust headset	52

Problem/symptom	Cause	Remedy	Page
Rim brake defective	1. brake needs adjusting	correct and align	101
	2. rim greasy, wet or damaged	clean, straighten (or replace) rim	95
	3. brake cable pinched or corroded	free, lubricate	104f
	4. brake lever damaged	free, lubricate	104f
Rim brake squeals	1. brake block greasy or damaged	scrape or sand brake block	101f
	2. rim dirty or damaged	clean, straighten or replace	95
	3. brake arm loose	tighten pivot bolt	104
Coaster brake ineffective	1. chain loose or broken	adjust chain, move wheel forward	75f, 108
	2. brake counter lever loose	reinstall lever on chain stay	108
Llight defective (generator or battery operated)	1. generator roller slips off tire	align and bend to increase pressure	111f
	2. bulb defective	replace bulb	111f
	3. (generator) wiring or mass contact defective	remake contact	111f
	4. battery dead	replace battery	111f

Bibliography

Ballantine, R. *Richard's Bicycle Book*. New York: Ballantine; London: Pan, 1978.

Coles, C. W., and Glenn, H. T. *Glenn's Complete Bicycle Manual*. New York: Crown Publishers, 1973.

Cuthberson, T. *Anybody's Bike Book*. Berkeley: Ten Speed Press, 1976.

DeLong, F. *DeLong's Guide to Bicycles and Bicycling*. Radnor, PA: Chilton Books, 1983.

Langley, J. *The New Bike Book*. San Francisco: Bicycle Books, 1990.

Sloane, E. A. *Eugene A. Sloane's Complete Guide to All-Terrain Bicycles*. New York: Simon & Schuster. 1985.

Van der Plas, R. *The Bicycle Repair Book*. San Francisco: Bicycle Books, 1985.

—. *Mountain Bike Maintenance*. San Francisco: Bicycle Books, 1989.

Index

Bicycle Books Publications

The New Bike Book

How to make the most of your new bicycle
by Jim Langley

This non-technical book provides down-to-earth advice for the novice bicycle owner on how to enjoy the sport without getting bogged down in too many technical details.

6 x 4$^{1}/_{2}$ inches (horizontal format), softcover, 128 pages with 50 line drawings.
ISBN 0-933201-28-8
US price $4.95

The Mountain Bike Book

Choosing, riding and maintaining the off-road bicycle
by Rob Van der Plas

The first and still the most authoritative book ever published about the modern mountain bike, or ATB, now fully updated. Shows how to select, equip, ride and maintain this wonderful machine. Lavishly illustrated and clearly written, this is the most useful *accessory* for any mountain bike rider.

ISBN 0-933201-32-X
6 x 9 inches, soft cover, 208 pages, with 300 photos
and line drawings.
US price $9.95

The Bicycle Repair Book

The complete manual of bicycle care
by Rob Van der Plas

The most thorough and systematic bicycle repair
manual on the market today. It covers all repair and
maintenance jobs required on any kind of bicycle. Complete with step-by-step instructions, clear illustrations
and an extensive troubleshooting guide.

6 x 9 inches, soft cover, 144 pages, with 300
illustrations.
ISBN 0-933201-11-7
US price $8.95

Mountain Bike Maintenance

Repairing and maintaining the off-road bicycle
by Rob Van der Plas

A practical repair and maintenance guide for the mountain bike rider. Covers all essential operations in clearly illustrated step-by-step instructions.

6 x 9 inches, soft cover, softcover, 112 pages, with 150 line drawings.
ISBN 0-933201-22-2
US price $7.95

The Bicycle Racing Guide

Technique and training for bike racers and triathletes
by Rob Van der Plas

The most concise and useful book for those who want to increase their cycling speed. Includes an introduction to the sport, as well as complete instructions for scientific training methods and practical advice for racing and training situations.

6 x 9 inches, soft cover, 256 pages, with 250 photographs and line drawings.
ISBN 0-933201-13-3
US price $10.95

The Bicycle Touring Manual

Using the bike for touring and camping
by Rob Van der Plas

Easily the most useful book for the cyclist who plans to travel by bike. This thorough and well illustrated manual systematically shows you how to select, use and maintain the equipment, how to plan your tour and how to enjoy cycling at home and abroad.

6 x 9 inches, soft cover, 272 pages, with 80 photographs and 180 line drawings.
ISBN 0-933201-15-X
US price $10.95

The Bicycle Commuting Book

Using the bicycle for utility and transportation
by Rob Van der Plas

A practical manual for the use of the bicycle as a means of transport. Covers in details all relevant topics, ranging from equipment selection to safety in an urban environment.

6 x 9 inches, soft cover, 128 pages, with 100 photos and line drawings.
US edition: ISBN 0-933201-19-2; $7.95)
UK edition: ISBN 0-933201-29-X; £4.95

In High Gear

The world of professional bicycle racing
by Samuel Abt

A fascinating account of the life of the professional bicycle racer. Get to know the men and women who work at 'the hardest job in the world. Expanded and up-dated to Include LeMond's 1989 Tour victory.

6 x 9 inches, 208 pages text plus 16-page photo insert with 40 photos
Hardcover: ISBN 0-933201-33-8; US price $18.95,
Paperback: ISBN 0-933201-34-6; US price $10.95

Bicycle Fuel

Nutrition for bicycle riders
by Richard Rafoth MD

A complete, easy-to-read but scientifically founded manual on nutrition for bicycle riders. Particularly useful for long distance riders and all who ride in pursuit of fitness or competition.

6 x 9 inches, soft cover, 128 pages, with 30 photos and line drawings.
ISBN 0-933201-17-6
US price $7.95

Major Taylor

The extraordinary career of a champion bicycle racer
by Andrew Ritchie

Beautifully illustrated and vividly told, this is the authentic story of the dramatic life of one of the earliest great black American athletes. Bicycle racer Major Taylor vanquished his competitors at home and abroad some eighty years before Greg LeMond became the first American to win the Tour de France

6 x 9 inches, hard cover, 304 pages text plus
32-page photo insert with 70 photographs.
ISBN 0-933201-14-1
US price $19.95

The Bicycle Fitness Book

Riding the bike for health and fitness
by Rob Van der Plas

A comprehensive guide to cycling for fitness, including topics ranging from equipment selection to nutrition and riding techniques.

6 x 9 inches, soft cover, 144 pages, with 120 illustrations.
ISBN 0-933201-23-0
US price $7.95

Book Ordering Form

All books published by Bicycle Books, Inc. may be obtained through the book or bike trade. If not available locally, order directly from the publisher. Allow three weeks for delivery. Fill out both sides of coupon and mail to:

Bicycle Books, Inc.
PO Box 2038
Mill Valley CA 94941 (USA)

Please include payment in full (check or money order payable to Bicycle Books, Inc.). If not paid in advance, books will be sent UPS COD.

Canadian and other foreign customers please note: Prices quoted are in US Dollars. Postage and handling fee for foreign orders is $2.50 per book. Payment in US currency (enquire at your bank) must be enclosed — no COD available.

Sub Total (enter amount from reverse of form): $ _____
California residents add 6.5% tax: $ _____
Shipping and handling $1.50 per book: $ _____

Total amount (pay this amount):   **$** _____

Name: _____

Address: _____

City, state, zip _____   Tel.: (____) _____

Charge to VISA/MC No. _____ Signature _____

Book Ordering Form (please fill out both sides)

☐ Check here
if payment enclosed

Please send the following books:

The Mountain Bike Book	____ copies @	$9.95	=	$ _____
The Bicycle Repair Book	____ copies @	$8.95	=	$ _____
The Bicycle Racing Guide	____ copies @	$10.95	=	$ _____
The Bicycle Touring Manual	____ copies @	$10.95	=	$ _____
Roadside Bicycle Repairs	____ copies @	$4.95	=	$ _____
Major Taylor (hardcover)	____ copies @	$19.95	=	$ _____
Bicycling Fuel	____ copies @	$7.95	=	$ _____
Mountain Bike Maintenance	____ copies @	$7.95	=	$ _____
In High Gear(hardcover)	____ copies @	$18.95	=	$ _____
In High Gear(softcover)	____ copies @	$10.95	=	$ _____
The Bicycle Fitness Book	____ copies @	$7.95	=	$ _____
The Bicycle Commuting Book	____ copies @	$7.95	=	$ _____
The New Bike Book	____ copies @	$4.95	=	$ _____
Bicycle Technology	____ copies @	$14.95	=	$ _____

Sub Total (transfer to reverse of form): $ _____

Bicycle Books, Inc., PO Box 2038, Mill Valley CA 94941, Tel. (415) 381 0172